All of Grace

By Charles Haddon Spurgeon
This Edition Edited by Anthony Uyl

Woodstock, Ontario, Canada 2017

All of Grace
By Charles Haddon Spurgeon (1834-1892)
This Edition Edited by Anthony Uyl

An Earnest Word with Those Who Are Seeking Salvation
by the Lord Jesus Christ

"Where sin abounded, grace did much more abound." Romans 5:20

The text of All of Grace is all in the Public Domain. The layout and Devoted Publishing logo are Copyright ©2017 Devoted Publishing. This edition is published by Devoted Publishing a division of 2165467 Ontario Inc.

**What kind of philosophies do you have?
Let us know!**

Visit our online store: www.devotedpublishing.com
Contact us at: devotedpub@hotmail.com
Visit us on Facebook: @DevotedPublishing

Published in Woodstock, Ontario, Canada 2017

For bulk educational rates, please contact us at the above email address.

ISBN: 978-1-77356-147-9

Table of Contents

- TO YOU ... 4
- WHAT ARE WE AT? ... 5
- GOD JUSTIFIETH THE UNGODLY ... 6
- "IT IS GOD THAT JUSTIFIETH" ... 9
- JUST AND THE JUSTIFIER ... 12
- CONCERNING DELIVERANCE FROM SINNING ... 14
- BY GRACE THROUGH FAITH ... 17
- FAITH, WHAT IS IT? ... 18
- HOW MAY FAITH BE ILLUSTRATED? ... 20
- WHY ARE WE SAVED BY FAITH? ... 23
- ALAS! I CAN DO NOTHING! ... 25
- THE INCREASE OF FAITH ... 30
- REGENERATION AND THE HOLY SPIRIT ... 32
- "MY REDEEMER LIVETH" ... 34
- REPENTANCE MUST GO WITH FORGIVENESS ... 36
- HOW REPENTANCE IS GIVEN ... 39
- THE FEAR OF FINAL FALLING ... 41
- CONFIRMATION ... 43
- WHY SAINTS PERSEVERE ... 45
- CLOSE ... 47

TO YOU

HE WHO SPOKE and wrote this message will be greatly disappointed if it does not lead many to the Lord Jesus. It is sent forth in childlike dependence upon the power of God the Holy Ghost, to use it in the conversion of millions, if so He pleases. No doubt many poor men and women will take up this little volume, and the Lord will visit them with grace. To answer this end, the very plainest language has been chosen, and many homely expressions have been used. But if those of wealth and rank should glance at this book, the Holy Ghost can impress them also; since that which can be understood by the unlettered is none the less attractive to the instructed. Oh that some might read it who will become great winners of souls!

Who knows how many will find their way to peace by what they read here? A more important question to you, dear reader, is this- -Will you be one of them?

A certain man placed a fountain by the wayside, and he hung up a cup near to it by a little chain. He was told some time after that a great art-critic had found much fault with its design. "But," said he, "do many thirsty persons drink at it?" Then they told him that thousands of poor people, men, women, and children, slaked their thirst at this fountain; and he smiled and said, that he was little troubled by the critic's observation, only he hoped that on some sultry summer's day the critic himself might fill the cup, and be refreshed, and praise the name of the Lord.

Here is my fountain, and here is my cup: find fault if you please; but do drink of the water of life. I only care for this. I had rather bless the soul of the poorest crossing-sweeper, or rag-gatherer, than please a prince of the blood, and fail to convert him to God.

Reader, do you mean business in reading these pages? If so, we are agreed at the outset; but nothing short of your finding Christ and Heaven is the business aimed at here. Oh that we may seek this together! I do so by dedicating this little book with prayer. Will not you join me by looking up to God, and asking Him to bless you while you read? Providence has put these pages in your way, you have a little spare time in which to read them, and you feel willing to give your attention to them. These are good signs. Who knows but the set time of blessing is come for you? At any rate, "The Holy Ghost saith, Today, if ye will hear his voice, harden not your hearts."

WHAT ARE WE AT?

I HEARD A STORY; I think it came from the North Country: A minister called upon a poor woman, intending to give her help; for he knew that she was very poor. With his money in his hand, he knocked at the door; but she did not answer. He concluded she was not at home, and went his way. A little after he met her at the church, and told her that he had remembered her need: "I called at your house, and knocked several times, and I suppose you were not at home, for I had no answer." "At what hour did you call, sir?" "It was about noon." "Oh, dear," she said, "I heard you, sir, and I am so sorry I did not answer; but I thought it was the man calling for the rent." Many a poor woman knows what this meant. Now, it is my desire to be heard, and therefore I want to say that I am not calling for the rent; indeed, it is not the object of this book to ask anything of you, but to tell you that salvation is all of grace, which means, free, gratis, for nothing.

Oftentimes, when we are anxious to win attention, our hearer thinks, "Ah! now I am going to be told my duty. It is the man calling for that which is due to God, and I am sure I have nothing wherewith to pay. I will not be at home." No, this book does not come to make a demand upon you, but to bring you something. We are not going to talk about law, and duty, and punishment, but about love, and goodness, and forgiveness, and mercy, and eternal life. Do not, therefore, act as if you were not at home: do not turn a deaf ear, or a careless heart. I am asking nothing of you in the name of God or man. It is not my intent to make any requirement at your hands; but I come in God's name, to bring you a free gift, which it shall be to your present and eternal joy to receive. Open the door, and let my pleadings enter. "Come now, and let us reason together." The Lord himself invites you to a conference concerning your immediate and endless happiness, and He would not have done this if He did not mean well toward you. Do not refuse the Lord Jesus who knocks at your door; for He knocks with a hand which was nailed to the tree for such as you are. Since His only and sole object is your good, incline your ear and come to Him. Hearken diligently, and let the good word sink into your soul. It may be that the hour is come in which you shall enter upon that new life which is the beginning of heaven. Faith cometh by hearing, and reading is a sort of hearing: faith may come to you while you are reading this book. Why not? O blessed Spirit of all grace, make it so!

GOD JUSTIFIETH THE UNGODLY

THIS MESSAGE is for you. You will find the text in the Epistle to the Romans, in the fourth chapter and the fifth verse:

To him that worketh not, but believeth on him that justifieth the ungodly, his faith is counted for righteousness.

I call your attention to those words, "Him that justifieth the ungodly." They seem to me to be very wonderful words.

Are you not surprised that there should be such an expression as that in the Bible, "That justifieth the ungodly?" I have heard that men that hate the doctrines of the cross bring it as a charge against God, that He saves wicked men and receives to Himself the vilest of the vile. See how this Scripture accepts the charge, and plainly states it! By the mouth of His servant Paul, by the inspiration of the Holy Ghost, He takes to Himself the title of "Him that justifieth the ungodly." He makes those just who are unjust, forgives those who deserve to be punished, and favors those who deserve no favor. You thought, did you not, that salvation was for the good? that God's grace was for the pure and holy, who are free from sin? It has fallen into your mind that, if you were excellent, then God would reward you; and you have thought that because you are not worthy, therefore there could be no way of your enjoying His favor. You must be somewhat surprised to read a text like this: "Him that justifieth the ungodly." I do not wonder that you are surprised; for with all my familiarity with the great grace of God, I never cease to wonder at it. It does sound surprising, does it not, that it should be possible for a holy God to justify an unholy man? We, according to the natural legality of our hearts, are always talking about our own goodness and our own worthiness, and we stubbornly hold to it that there must be somewhat in us in order to win the notice of God. Now, God, who sees through all deceptions, knows that there is no goodness whatever in us. He says that "there is none righteous, no not one." He knows that "all our righteousnesses are as filthy rags," and, therefore the Lord Jesus did not come into the world to look after goodness and righteousness with him, and to bestow them upon persons who have none of them. He comes, not because we are just, but to make us so: he justifieth the ungodly.

When a counsellor comes into court, if he is an honest man, he desires to plead the case of an innocent person and justify him before the court from the things which are falsely laid to his charge. It should be the lawyer's object to justify the innocent person, and he should not attempt to screen the guilty party. It lies not in man's right nor in man's power truly to justify the guilty. This is a miracle reserved for the Lord alone. God, the infinitely just Sovereign, knows that there is not a just man upon earth that doeth good and sinneth not, and therefore, in the infinite sovereignty of His divine nature and in the splendor of His ineffable love, He undertakes the task, not so much of justifying the just as of justifying the ungodly. God has devised ways and means of making the ungodly man to stand justly accepted before Him: He has set up a system by which with perfect justice He can treat the guilty as if he had been all his life free from offence, yea, can treat him as if he were wholly free from sin. He justifieth the ungodly.

Jesus Christ came into the world to save sinners. It is a very surprising thing--a thing to be marveled at most of all by those who enjoy it. I know that it is to me even to this day the greatest wonder that I ever heard of, that God should ever justify me. I feel myself to be a lump of unworthiness, a mass of corruption, and a heap of sin, apart from His almighty love. I know by a full assurance that I am justified by faith which is in Christ Jesus, and treated as if I had been perfectly just, and made an heir of God and a joint heir with Christ; and yet by nature I must take my place among the most sinful. I, who am altogether undeserving, am treated as if I had been deserving. I am loved with as much love as if I had always been godly, whereas aforetime I was ungodly. Who can help being astonished at this? Gratitude for such favor stands dressed in robes of wonder.

Now, while this is very surprising, I want you to notice how available it makes the gospel to you and to me. If God justifieth the ungodly, then, dear friend, He can justify you. Is not that the very kind of person that you are? If you are unconverted at this moment, it is a very proper description of you; you have lived without God, you have been the reverse of godly; in one word, you have been and are ungodly. Perhaps you have not even attended a place of worship on Sunday, but have lived in disregard of God's day, and house, and Word--this proves you to have been ungodly. Sadder still, it may be you have even tried to doubt God's existence, and have gone the length of saying that you did so. You have lived on this fair earth, which is full of the tokens of God's presence, and all the while you have shut your eyes to the clear evidences of His power and Godhead. You have lived as if there were no God. Indeed, you would have been very pleased if you could have demonstrated to yourself to a certainty that there was no God whatever. Possibly you have lived a great many years in this way, so that you are now pretty well settled in your ways, and yet God is not in any of them. If you were labeled UNGODLY it would as well describe you as if the sea were to be labeled salt water. Would it not?

Possibly you are a person of another sort; you have regularly attended to all the outward forms of religion, and yet you have had no heart in them at all, but have been really ungodly. Though meeting with the people of God, you have never met with God for yourself; you have been in the choir, and yet have not praised the Lord with your heart. You have lived without any love to God in your heart, or regard to his commands in your life. Well, you are just the kind of man to whom this gospel is sent--this gospel which says that God justifieth the ungodly. It is very wonderful, but it is happily available for you. It just suits you. Does it not? How I wish that you would accept it! If you are a sensible man, you will see the remarkable grace of God in providing for such as you are, and you will say to yourself, "Justify the ungodly! Why, then, should not I be justified, and justified at once?"

Now, observe further, that it must be so--that the salvation of God is for those who do not deserve it, and have no preparation for it. It is reasonable that the statement should be put in the Bible; for, dear friend, no others need justifying but those who have no justification of their own. If any of my readers are perfectly righteous, they want no justifying. You feel that you are doing your duty well, and almost putting heaven under an obligation to you. What do you want with a Saviour, or with mercy? What do you want with justification? You will be tired of my book by this time, for it will have no interest to you.

If any of you are giving yourselves such proud airs, listen to me for a little while. You will be lost, as sure as you are alive. You righteous men, whose righteousness is all of your own working, are either deceivers or deceived; for the Scripture cannot lie, and it saith plainly, "There is none righteous, no, not one." In any case I have no gospel to preach to the self-righteous, no, not a word of it. Jesus Christ himself came not to call the righteous, and I am not going to do what He did not do. If I called you, you would not come, and, therefore, I will not call you, under that character. No, I bid you rather look at that righteousness of yours till you see what a delusion it is. It is not half so substantial as a cobweb. Have done with it! Flee from it! Oh believe that the only persons that can need justification are those who are not in themselves just! They need that something should be done for them to make them just before the judgment seat of God. Depend upon it, the Lord only does that which is needful. Infinite wisdom never attempts that which is unnecessary. Jesus never undertakes that which is superfluous. To make him just who is just is no work for God--that were a labor for a fool; but to make him just who is unjust--that is work for infinite love and mercy. To justify the ungodly--this is a miracle worthy of a God. And for certain it is so.

Now, look. If there be anywhere in the world a physician who has discovered sure and precious remedies, to whom is that physician sent? To those who are perfectly healthy? I think not. Put him down in a district where there are no sick persons, and he feels that he is not in his place. There is nothing for him to do. "The whole have no need of a physician, but they that are sick." Is it not equally clear that the great remedies of grace and redemption are for the sick in soul? They cannot be for the whole, for they cannot be of use to such. If you, dear friend, feel that you are spiritually sick, the Physician has come into the world for you. If you are altogether undone by reason of your sin, you are the very person aimed at in the plan of salvation. I say that the Lord of love had just such as you are in His eye when He arranged the system of grace. Suppose a man of generous spirit were to resolve to forgive all those who were indebted to him; it is clear that this can only apply to those really in his debt. One person owes him a thousand pounds; another owes him fifty pounds; each one has but to have his bill receipted, and the liability is wiped out. But the most generous person cannot forgive the debts of those who do not owe him anything. It is out of the power of Omnipotence to forgive where there is no sin. Pardon, therefore, cannot be for you who have no sin. Pardon must be for the guilty. Forgiveness must be for the sinful. It were absurd to talk of forgiving those who do not need forgiveness-- pardoning those who have never offended.

Do you think that you must be lost because you are a sinner? This is the reason why you can be saved. Because you own yourself to be a sinner I would encourage you to believe that grace is ordained for such as you are. One of our hymn-writers even dared to say:

A sinner is a sacred thing;
The Holy Ghost hath made him so.

All of Grace

It is truly so, that Jesus seeks and saves that which is lost. He died and made a real atonement for real sinners. When men are not playing with words, or calling themselves "miserable sinners," out of mere compliment, I feel overjoyed to meet with them. I would be glad to talk all night to bona fide sinners. The inn of mercy never closes its doors upon such, neither weekdays nor Sunday. Our Lord Jesus did not die for imaginary sins, but His heart's blood was spilt to wash out deep crimson stains, which nothing else can remove.

He that is a black sinner--he is the kind of man that Jesus Christ came to make white. A gospel preacher on one occasion preached a sermon from, "Now also the axe is laid to the root of the trees," and he delivered such a sermon that one of his hearers said to him, "One would have thought that you had been preaching to criminals. Your sermon ought to have been delivered in the county jail." "Oh, no," said the good man, "if I were preaching in the county jail, I should not preach from that text, there I should preach 'This is a faithful saying, and worthy of all acceptation, that Christ Jesus came into the world to save sinners.'" Just so. The law is for the self-righteous, to humble their pride: the gospel is for the lost, to remove their despair.

If you are not lost, what do you want with a Saviour? Should the shepherd go after those who never went astray? Why should the woman sweep her house for the bits of money that were never out of her purse? No, the medicine is for the diseased; the quickening is for the dead; the pardon is for the guilty; liberation is for those who are bound: the opening of eyes is for those who are blind. How can the Saviour, and His death upon the cross, and the gospel of pardon, be accounted for, unless it be upon the supposition that men are guilty and worthy of condemnation? The sinner is the gospel's reason for existence. You, my friend, to whom this word now comes, if you are undeserving, ill-deserving, hell-deserving, you are the sort of man for whom the gospel is ordained, and arranged, and proclaimed. God justifieth the ungodly.

I would like to make this very plain. I hope that I have done so already; but still, plain as it is, it is only the Lord that can make a man see it. It does at first seem most amazing to an awakened man that salvation should really be for him as a lost and guilty one. He thinks that it must be for him as a penitent man, forgetting that his penitence is a part of his salvation. "Oh," says he, "but I must be this and that,"--all of which is true, for he shall be this and that as the result of salvation; but salvation comes to him before he has any of the results of salvation. It comes to him, in fact, while he deserves only this bare, beggarly, base, abominable description, "ungodly." That is all he is when God's gospel comes to justify him.

May I, therefore, urge upon any who have no good thing about them--who fear that they have not even a good feeling, or anything whatever that can recommend them to God--that they will firmly believe that our gracious God is able and willing to take them without anything to recommend them, and to forgive them spontaneously, not because they are good, but because He is good. Does He not make His sun to shine on the evil as well as on the good? Does He not give fruitful seasons, and send the rain and the sunshine in their time upon the most ungodly nations? Ay, even Sodom had its sun, and Gomorrah had its dew. Oh friend, the great grace of God surpasses my conception and your conception, and I would have you think worthily of it! As high as the heavens are above the earth; so high are God's thoughts above our thoughts. He can abundantly pardon. Jesus Christ came into the world to save sinners: forgiveness is for the guilty.

Do not attempt to touch yourself up and make yourself something other than you really are; but come as you are to Him who justifies the ungodly. A great artist some short time ago had painted a part of the corporation of the city in which he lived, and he wanted, for historic purposes, to include in his picture certain characters well known in the town. A crossing-sweeper, unkempt, ragged, filthy, was known to everybody, and there was a suitable place for him in the picture. The artist said to this ragged and rugged individual, "I will pay you well if you will come down to my studio and let me take your likeness." He came round in the morning, but he was soon sent about his business; for he had washed his face, and combed his hair, and donned a respectable suit of clothes. He was needed as a beggar, and was not invited in any other capacity. Even so, the gospel will receive you into its halls if you come as a sinner, not otherwise. Wait not for reformation, but come at once for salvation. God justifieth the ungodly, and that takes you up where you now are: it meets you in your worst estate.

Come in your deshabille. I mean, come to your heavenly Father in all your sin and sinfulness. Come to Jesus just as you are, leprous, filthy, naked, neither fit to live nor fit to die. Come, you that are the very sweepings of creation; come, though you hardly dare to hope for anything but death. Come, though despair is brooding over you, pressing upon your bosom like a horrible nightmare. Come and ask the Lord to justify another ungodly one. Why should He not? Come for this great mercy of God is meant for such as you are. I put it in the language of the text, and I cannot put it more strongly: the Lord God Himself takes to Himself this gracious title, "Him that justifieth the ungodly." He makes just, and causes to be treated as just, those who by nature are ungodly. Is not that a wonderful word for you? Reader, do not delay till you have well considered this matter.

"IT IS GOD THAT JUSTIFIETH"
- Romans 8:33

A WONDERFUL THING it is, this being justified, or made just. If we had never broken the laws of God we should not have needed it, for we should have been just in ourselves. He who has all his life done the things which he ought to have done, and has never done anything which he ought not to have done, is justified by the law. But you, dear reader, are not of that sort, I am quite sure. You have too much honesty to pretend to be without sin, and therefore you need to be justified.

Now, if you justify yourself, you will simply be a self-deceiver. Therefore do not attempt it. It is never worth while.

If you ask your fellow mortals to justify you, what can they do? You can make some of them speak well of you for small favors, and others will backbite you for less. Their judgment is not worth much.

Our text says, "It is God that justifieth," and this is a deal more to the point. It is an astonishing fact, and one that we ought to consider with care. Come and see.

In the first place, nobody else but God would ever have thought of justifying those who are guilty. They have lived in open rebellion; they have done evil with both hands; they have gone from bad to worse; they have turned back to sin even after they have smarted for it, and have therefore for a while been forced to leave it. They have broken the law, and trampled on the gospel. They have refused proclamations of mercy, and have persisted in ungodliness. How can they be forgiven and justified? Their fellowmen, despairing of them, say, "They are hopeless cases." Even Christians look upon them with sorrow rather than with hope. But not so their God. He, in the splendor of his electing grace having chosen some of them before the foundation of the world, will not rest till He has justified them, and made them to be accepted in the Beloved. Is it not written, "Whom he did predestinate, them he also called: and whom he called them he also justified: and whom he justified, them he also glorified"? Thus you see there are some whom the Lord resolves to justify: why should not you and I be of the number?

None but God would ever have thought of justifying me. I am a wonder to myself. I doubt not that grace is equally seen in others. Look at Saul of Tarsus, who foamed at the mouth, against God's servants. Like a hungry wolf, he worried the lambs and the sheep right and left; and yet God struck him down on the road to Damascus, and changed his heart, and so fully justified him that ere long, this man became the greatest preacher of justification by faith that ever lived. He must often have marveled that he was justified by faith in Christ Jesus; for he was once a determined stickler for salvation by the works of the law. None but God would have ever thought of justifying such a man as Saul the persecutor; but the Lord God is glorious in grace.

But, even if anybody had thought of justifying the ungodly, none but God could have done it. It is quite impossible for any person to forgive offences which have not been committed against himself. A person has greatly injured you; you can forgive him, and I hope you will; but no third person can forgive him apart from you. If the wrong is done to you, the pardon must come from you. If we have sinned against God, it is in God's power to forgive; for the sin is against Himself. That is why David says, in the fifty-first Psalm: "Against thee, thee only, have I sinned, and done this evil in thy sight"; for then God, against whom the offence is committed, can put the offence away. That which we owe to God, our great Creator can remit, if so it pleases Him; and if He remits it, it is remitted. None but the great God, against whom we have committed the sin, can blot out that sin; let us, therefore, see that we go to Him and seek mercy at His hands. Do not let us be led aside by those who would have us confess to them; they have no warrant in the Word of God for their pretensions. But even if they were ordained to pronounce absolution in God's name, it must still be better to go ourselves to the great Lord through Jesus Christ, the Mediator, and seek and find pardon at His hand; since we are sure that this is the right way. Proxy religion involves too great a risk: you had better see to your soul's matters yourself, and leave them in no man's hands.

Only God can justify the ungodly; but He can do it to perfection. He casts our sins behind His back, He blots them out; He says that though they be sought for, they shall not be found. With no other reason for it but His own infinite goodness, He has prepared a glorious way by which He can make scarlet sins as white as snow, and remove our transgressions from us as far as the east is from the west. He says, "I will not remember your sins." He goes the length of making an end of sin. One of old called out in amazement, "Who is a God like unto thee, that pardoneth iniquity, and passeth by the transgression of the remnant of his heritage? he retaineth not his anger for ever, because he delighteth in mercy" (Micah 7:18).

We are not now speaking of justice, nor of God's dealing with men according to their deserts. If you profess to deal with the righteous Lord on law terms, everlasting wrath threatens you, for that is what you deserve. Blessed be His name, He has not dealt with us after our sins; but now He treats with us on terms of free grace and infinite compassion, and He says, "I will receive you graciously, and love you freely." Believe it, for it is certainly true that the great God is able to treat the guilty with abundant mercy; yea, He is able to treat the ungodly as if they had been always godly. Read carefully the parable of the prodigal son, and see how the forgiving father received the returning wanderer with as much love as if he had never gone away, and had never defiled himself with harlots. So far did he carry this that the elder brother began to grumble at it; but the father never withdrew his love. Oh my brother, however guilty you may be, if you will only come back to your God and Father, He will treat you as if you had never done wrong! He will regard you as just, and deal with you accordingly. What say you to this?

Do you not see--for I want to bring this out clearly, what a splendid thing it is--that as none but God would think of justifying the ungodly, and none but God could do it, yet the Lord can do it? See how the apostle puts the challenge, "Who shall lay anything to the charge of God's elect? It is God that justifieth." If God has justified a man it is well done, it is rightly done, it is justly done, it is everlastingly done. I read a statement in a magazine which is full of venom against the gospel and those who preach it, that we hold some kind of theory by which we imagine that sin can be removed from men. We hold no theory, we publish a fact. The grandest fact under heaven is this-- that Christ by His precious blood does actually put away sin, and that God, for Christ's sake, dealing with men on terms of divine mercy, forgives the guilty and justifies them, not according to anything that He sees in them, or foresees will be in them, but according to the riches of His mercy which lie in His own heart. This we have preached, do preach, and will preach as long as we live. "It is God that justifieth"--that justifieth the ungodly; He is not ashamed of doing it, nor are we of preaching it.

The justification which comes from God himself must be beyond question. If the Judge acquits me, who can condemn me? If the highest court in the universe has pronounced me just, who shall lay anything to my charge? Justification from God is a sufficient answer to an awakened conscience. The Holy Spirit by its means breathes peace over our entire nature, and we are no longer afraid. With this justification we can answer all the roarings and railings of Satan and ungodly men. With this we shall be able to die: with this we shall boldly rise again, and face the last great assize.

> Bold shall I stand in that great day,
> For who aught to my charge shall lay?
> While by my Lord absolved I am
> From sin's tremendous curse and blame.

Friend, the Lord can blot out all your sins. I make no shot in the dark when I say this. "All manner of sin and of blasphemy shall be forgiven unto men." Though you are steeped up to your throat in crime, He can with a word remove the defilement, and say, "I will, be thou clean." The Lord is a great forgiver.

"I believe in the Forgiveness of Sins." Do You?

He can even at this hour pronounce the sentence, "Thy sins be forgiven thee; go in peace;" and if He do this, no power in Heaven, or earth, or under the earth, can put you under suspicion, much less under wrath. Do not doubt the power of Almighty love. You could not forgive your fellow man had he offended you as you have offended God; but you must not measure God's corn with your bushel; His thoughts and ways are as much above yours as the heavens are high above the earth.

"Well," say you, "it would be a great miracle if the Lord were to pardon me." Just so. It would be a supreme miracle, and therefore He is likely to do it; for He does "great things and unsearchable" which we looked not for.

I was myself stricken down with a horrible sense of guilt, which made my life a misery to me; but when I heard the command, "Look unto me, and be ye saved, all the ends of the earth, for I am God and there is none else"--I looked, and in a moment the Lord justified me. Jesus Christ, made sin for me, was what I saw, and that sight gave me rest. When those who were bitten by the fiery serpents in the wilderness looked to the serpent of brass they were healed at once; and so was I when I looked to the crucified Saviour. The Holy Spirit, who enabled me to believe, gave me peace through believing. I felt as sure that I was forgiven, as before I felt sure of condemnation. I had been certain of my condemnation because the Word of God declared it, and my conscience bore witness to it; but when the Lord justified me I was made equally certain by the same witnesses. The word of the Lord in the Scripture saith, "He that believeth on him is not condemned," and my conscience bears witness that I believed, and that God in pardoning me is just. Thus I have the witness of the Holy Spirit and my own conscience, and these two agree in one. Oh, how I wish that my reader would receive the testimony of God upon this matter, and then full soon he would also have the witness in himself!

I venture to say that a sinner justified by God stands on even a surer footing than a righteous man justified by his works, if such there be. We could never be surer that we had done enough works; conscience would always be uneasy lest, after all, we should come short, and we could only have the trembling verdict of a fallible judgment to rely upon; but when God himself justifies, and the Holy Spirit bears witness thereto by giving us peace with God, why then we feel that the matter is sure and settled, and we enter into rest. No tongue can tell the depth of that calm which comes over the soul which has received the peace of God which passeth all understanding.

JUST AND THE JUSTIFIER

WE HAVE SEEN the ungodly justified, and have considered the great truth, that only God can justify any man; we now come a step further and make the inquiry--How can a just God justify guilty men? Here we are met with a full answer in the words of Paul, in Romans 3:21-26. We will read six verses from the chapter so as to get the run of the passage:

"But now the righteousness of God without the law is manifested, being witnessed by the law and the prophets; even the righteousness of God which is by faith of Jesus Christ unto all and upon all them that believe: for there is no difference; for all have sinned, and come short of the glory of God; being justified freely by his grace through the redemption that is in Christ Jesus: whom God hath set forth to be a propitiation through faith in his blood, to declare his righteousness for the remission of sins that are past, through the forbearance of God; to declare, I say, at this time his righteousness; that he might be just, and the justifier of him which believeth in Jesus."

Here suffer me to give you a bit of personal experience. When I was under the hand of the Holy Spirit, under conviction of sin, I had a clear and sharp sense of the justice of God. Sin, whatever it might be to other people, became to me an intolerable burden. It was not so much that I feared hell, but that I feared sin. I knew myself to be so horribly guilty that I remember feeling that if God did not punish me for sin He ought to do so. I felt that the Judge of all the earth ought to condemn such sin as mine. I sat on the judgment seat, and I condemned myself to perish; for I confessed that had I been God I could have done no other than send such a guilty creature as I was down to the lowest hell. All the while, I had upon my mind a deep concern for the honor of God's name, and the integrity of His moral government. I felt that it would not satisfy my conscience if I could be forgiven unjustly. The sin I had committed must be punished. But then there was the question how God could be just, and yet justify me who had been so guilty. I asked my heart: "How can He be just and yet the justifier?" I was worried and wearied with this question; neither could I see any answer to it. Certainly, I could never have invented an answer which would have satisfied my conscience.

The doctrine of the atonement is to my mind one of the surest proofs of the divine inspiration of Holy Scripture. Who would or could have thought of the just Ruler dying for the unjust rebel? This is no teaching of human mythology, or dream of poetical imagination. This method of expiation is only known among men because it is a fact; fiction could not have devised it. God Himself ordained it; it is not a matter which could have been imagined.

I had heard the plan of salvation by the sacrifice of Jesus from my youth up; but I did not know any more about it in my innermost soul than if I had been born and bred a Hottentot. The light was there, but I was blind; it was of necessity that the Lord himself should make the matter plain to me. It came to me as a new revelation, as fresh as if I had never read in Scripture that Jesus was declared to be the propitiation for sins that God might be just. I believe it will have to come as a revelation to every newborn child of God whenever he sees it; I mean that glorious doctrine of the substitution of the Lord Jesus. I came to understand that salvation was possible through vicarious sacrifice; and that provision had been made in the first constitution and arrangement of things for such a substitution. I was made to see that He who is the Son of God, co-equal, and co- eternal with the Father, had of old been made the covenant Head of a chosen people that He might in that capacity suffer for them and save them. Inasmuch as our fall was not at the first a personal one, for we fell in our federal representative, the first Adam, it became possible for us to be recovered by a second representative, even by Him who has undertaken to be the covenant head of His people, so as to be their second Adam. I saw that ere I actually sinned I had fallen by my first father's sin; and I rejoiced that therefore it became possible in point of law for me to rise by a second head and representative. The fall by Adam left a loophole of escape; another Adam can undo the ruin made by the first. When I was anxious about the possibility of a just God pardoning me, I understood and saw by faith that He who is the Son of God became man, and in His own blessed person bore my sin in His own body on the tree. I saw the chastisement of my peace was laid on Him, and that with His stripes I was healed. Dear friend, have you ever seen that? Have you ever understood how God can be just to the full, not remitting penalty nor blunting the edge of the sword, and yet can be infinitely merciful, and can justify the ungodly who turn to Him? It was because the Son of God, supremely glorious in His matchless person, undertook to vindicate the law by bearing the sentence due to me, that therefore God is able to pass by my sin. The law of God was more vindicated by the death of Christ than it would have been had all transgressors been sent to Hell. For the Son of God to suffer for sin was a more glorious establishment of the government of God, than for the whole race to suffer.

Jesus has borne the death penalty on our behalf. Behold the wonder! There He hangs upon the cross! This is the greatest sight you will ever see. Son of God and Son of Man, there He hangs, bearing pains unutterable, the just for the unjust, to bring us to God. Oh, the glory of that sight! The innocent punished! The Holy One condemned! The Ever-blessed made a curse! The infinitely glorious put to a shameful death! The more I look at the sufferings of the Son of God, the more sure I am that they must meet my case. Why did He suffer, if not to turn aside the penalty from us? If, then, He turned it aside by His death, it is turned aside, and those who believe in Him need not fear it. It must be so, that since expiation is made, God is able to forgive without shaking the basis of His throne, or in the least degree blotting the statute book. Conscience gets a full answer to her tremendous question. The wrath of God against iniquity, whatever that may be, must be beyond all conception terrible. Well did Moses say, "Who knoweth the power of thine anger?" Yet when we hear the Lord of glory cry, "Why hast thou forsaken me?" and see Him yielding up the ghost, we feel that the justice of God has received abundant vindication by obedience so perfect and death so terrible, rendered by so divine a person. If God himself bows before His own law, what more can be done? There is more in the atonement by way of merit, than there is in all human sin by way of demerit.

The great gulf of Jesus' loving self-sacrifice can swallow up the mountains of our sins, all of them. For the sake of the infinite good of this one representative man, the Lord may well look with favor upon other men, however unworthy they may be in and of themselves. It was a miracle of miracles that the Lord Jesus Christ should stand in our stead and

> *Bear that we might never bear*
> *His Father's righteous ire.*

But he has done so. "It is finished." God will spare the sinner because He did not spare His Son. God can pass by your transgressions because He laid those transgressions upon His only begotten Son nearly two thousand years ago. If you believe in Jesus (that is the point), then your sins were carried away by Him who was the scapegoat for His people.

What is it to believe in Him? It is not merely to say, "He is God and the Saviour," but to trust Him wholly and entirely, and take Him for all your salvation from this time forth and forever--your Lord, your Master, your all. If you will have Jesus, He has you already. If you believe on Him, I tell you you cannot go to hell; for that were to make the sacrifice of Christ of none effect. It cannot be that a sacrifice should be accepted, and yet the soul should die for whom that sacrifice has been received. If the believing soul could be condemned, then why a sacrifice? If Jesus died in my stead, why should I die also? Every believer can claim that the sacrifice was actually made for him: by faith he has laid his hands on it, and made it his own, and therefore he may rest assured that he can never perish. The Lord would not receive this offering on our behalf, and then condemn us to die. The Lord cannot read our pardon written in the blood of His own Son, and then smite us. That were impossible. Oh that you may have grace given you at once to look away to Jesus and to begin at the beginning, even at Jesus, who is the Fountain-head of mercy to guilty man!

"He justifieth the ungodly." "It is God that justifieth," therefore, and for that reason only it can be done, and He does it through the atoning sacrifice of His divine Son. Therefore it can be justly done--so justly done that none will ever question it--so thoroughly done that in the last tremendous day, when heaven and earth shall pass away, there shall be none that shall deny the validity of the justification. "Who is he that condemneth? It is Christ that died. Who shall lay anything to the charge of God's elect? It is God that justifieth."

Now, poor soul! will you come into this lifeboat, just as you are? Here is safety from the wreck! Accept the sure deliverance. "I have nothing with me," say you. You are not asked to bring anything with you. Men who escape for their lives will leave even their clothes behind. Leap for it, just as you are.

I will tell you this thing about myself to encourage you. My sole hope for heaven lies in the full atonement made upon Calvary's cross for the ungodly. On that I firmly rely. I have not the shadow of a hope anywhere else. You are in the same condition as I am; for we neither of us have anything of our own worth as a ground of trust. Let us join hands and stand together at the foot of the cross, and trust our souls once for all to Him who shed His blood for the guilty. We will be saved by one and the same Saviour. If you perish trusting Him, I must perish too. What can I do more to prove my own confidence in the gospel which I set before you?

CONCERNING DELIVERANCE FROM SINNING

IN THIS PLACE I would say a plain word or two to those who understand the method of justification by faith which is in Christ Jesus, but whose trouble is that they cannot cease from sin. We can never be happy, restful, or spiritually healthy till we become holy. We must be rid of sin; but how is the riddance to be wrought? This is the life-or-death question of many. The old nature is very strong, and they have tried to curb and tame it; but it will not be subdued, and they find themselves, though anxious to be better, if anything growing worse than before. The heart is so hard, the will is so obstinate, the passions are so furious, the thoughts are so volatile, the imagination is so ungovernable, the desires are so wild, that the man feels that he has a den of wild beasts within him, which will eat him up sooner than be ruled by him. We may say of our fallen nature what the Lord said to Job concerning Leviathan: "Wilt thou play with him as with a bird? or wilt thou bind him for thy maidens?" A man might as well hope to hold the north wind in the hollow of his hand as expect to control by his own strength those boisterous powers which dwell within his fallen nature. This is a greater feat than any of the fabled labors of Hercules: God is wanted here.

"I could believe that Jesus would forgive sin," says one, "but then my trouble is that I sin again, and that I feel such awful tendencies to evil within me. As surely as a stone, if it be flung up into the air, soon comes down again to the ground, so do I, though I am sent up to heaven by earnest preaching, return again to my insensible state. Alas! I am easily fascinated with the basilisk eyes of sin, and am thus held as under a spell, so that I cannot escape from my own folly."

Dear friend, salvation would be a sadly incomplete affair if it did not deal with this part of our ruined estate. We want to be purified as well as pardoned. Justification without sanctification would not be salvation at all. It would call the leper clean, and leave him to die of his disease; if would forgive the rebellion and allow the rebel to remain an enemy to his king. It would remove the consequences but overlook the cause, and this would leave an endless and hopeless task before us. It would stop the stream for a time, but leave an open fountain of defilement, which would sooner or later break forth with increased power. Remember that the Lord Jesus came to take away sin in three ways; He came to remove the penalty of sin, the power of sin, and, at last, the presence of sin. At once you may reach to the second part--the power of sin may immediately be broken; and so you will be on the road to the third, namely, the removal of the presence of sin. "We know that he was manifested to take away our sins."

The angel said of our Lord, "Thou shalt call his name Jesus, for he shall save his people from their sins." Our Lord Jesus came to destroy in us the works of the devil. That which was said at our Lord's birth was also declared in His death; for when the soldier pierced His side forthwith came there out blood and water, to set forth the double cure by which we are delivered from the guilt and the defilement of sin.

If, however, you are troubled about the power of sin, and about the tendencies of your nature, as you well may be, here is a promise for you. Have faith in it, for it stands in that covenant of grace which is ordered in all things and sure. God, who cannot lie, has said in Ezekiel 36:26:

A new heart also will I give you, and a new spirit will I put within you: and I will take away the stony heart out of your flesh, and I will give you an heart of flesh.

You see, it is all "I will," and "I will." "I will give," and "I will take away." This is the royal style of the King of kings, who is able to accomplish all His will. No word of His shall ever fall to the ground.

The Lord knows right well that you cannot change your own heart, and cannot cleanse your own nature; but He also knows that He can do both. He can cause the Ethiopian to change his skin, and the leopard his spots. Hear this, and be astonished: He can create you a second time; He can cause you to be born again. This is a miracle of grace, but the Holy Ghost will perform it. It would be a very wonderful thing if one could stand at the foot of the Niagara Falls, and could speak a word which should make the river Niagara begin to run up stream, and leap up that great precipice over which it now rolls in stupendous force. Nothing but the power of God could achieve that marvel; but that would be more than a fit parallel to what would take place if the course of your nature were altogether reversed. All things are possible with God. He can reverse the direction of your desires and the current of your life, and instead of going downward from God, He can make your whole being tend upward toward God. That is, in fact, what the Lord has promised to do for all who are in the covenant; and we know from Scripture that all believers are in the covenant. Let me read the words again:

A new spirit will I put within you: and I will take away the stony heart out of your flesh, and will give an heart of flesh. (Ezekiel 11:19).

What a wonderful promise! And it is yea and amen in Christ Jesus to the glory of God by us. Let us lay hold of it; accept it as true, and appropriate it to ourselves. Then shall it be fulfilled in us, and we shall have, in after days and years, to sing of that wondrous change which the sovereign grace of God has wrought in us.

It is well worthy of consideration that when the Lord takes away the stony heart, that deed is done; and when that is once done, no known power can ever take away that new heart which He gives, and that right spirit which He puts within us. "The gifts and calling of God are without repentance"; that is, without repentance on His part; He does not take away what He once has given. Let Him renew you and you will be renewed. Man's reformations and cleanings up soon come to an end, for the dog returns to his vomit; but when God puts a new heart into us, the new heart is there forever, and never will it harden into stone again. He who made it flesh will keep it so. Herein we may rejoice and be glad forever in that which God creates in the kingdom of His grace.

To put the matter very simply--did you ever hear of Mr. Rowland Hill's illustration of the cat and the sow? I will give it in my own fashion, to illustrate our Saviour's expressive words--"Ye must be born again." Do you see that cat? What a cleanly creature she is! How cleverly she washes herself with her tongue and her paws! It is quite a pretty sight! Did you ever see a sow do that? No, you never did. It is contrary to its nature. It prefers to wallow in the mire. Go and teach a sow to wash itself, and see how little success you would gain. It would be a great sanitary improvement if swine would be clean. Teach them to wash and clean themselves as the cat has been doing! Useless task. You may by force wash that sow, but it hastens to the mire, and is soon as foul as ever. The only way in which you can get a sow to wash itself is to transform it into a cat; then it will wash and be clean, but not till then! Suppose that transformation to be accomplished, and then what was difficult or impossible is easy enough; the swine will henceforth be fit for your parlor and your hearth-rug. So it is with an ungodly man; you cannot force him to do what a renewed man does most willingly; you may teach him, and set him a good example, but he cannot learn the art of holiness, for he has no mind to it; his nature leads him another way. When the Lord makes a new man of him, then all things wear a different aspect. So great is this change, that I once heard a convert say, "Either all the world is changed, or else I am." The new nature follows after right as naturally as the old nature wanders after wrong. What a blessing to receive such a nature! Only the Holy Ghost can give it.

Did it ever strike you what a wonderful thing it is for the Lord to give a new heart and a right spirit to a man? You have seen a lobster, perhaps, which has fought with another lobster, and lost one of its claws, and a new claw has grown. That is a remarkable thing; but it is a much more astounding fact that a man should have a new heart given to him. This, indeed, is a miracle beyond the powers of nature. There is a tree. If you cut off one of its limbs, another one may grow in its place; but can you change the tree; can you sweeten sour sap; can you make the thorn bear figs? You can graft something better into it and that is the analogy which nature gives us of the work of grace; but absolutely to change the vital sap of the tree would be a miracle indeed. Such a prodigy and mystery of power God works in all who believe in Jesus.

If you yield yourself up to His divine working, the Lord will alter your nature; He will subdue the old nature, and breathe new life into you. Put your trust in the Lord Jesus Christ, and He will take the stony heart out of your flesh, and He will give you a heart of flesh. Where everything was hard, everything shall be tender; where everything was vicious, everything shall be virtuous: where everything tended downward, everything shall rise upward with impetuous force. The lion of anger shall give place to the lamb of meekness; the raven of uncleanness shall fly before the dove of purity; the vile serpent of deceit shall be trodden under the heel of truth.

I have seen with my own eyes such marvellous changes of moral and spiritual character that I despair of none. I could, if it were fitting, point out those who were once unchaste women who are now pure as the driven snow, and blaspheming men who now delight all around them by their intense devotion. Thieves are made honest, drunkards sober, liars truthful, and scoffers zealous. Wherever the grace of God has appeared to a man it has trained him to deny ungodliness and worldly lusts, and to live soberly, righteously, and godly in this present evil world: and, dear reader, it will do the same for you.

"I cannot make this change," says one. Who said you could? The Scripture which we have quoted speaks not of what man will do, but of what God will do. It is God's promise, and it is for

All of Grace

Him to fulfill His own engagements. Trust in Him to fulfill His Word to you, and it will be done.

"But how is it to be done?" What business is that of yours? Must the Lord explain His methods before you will believe him? The Lord's working in this matter is a great mystery: the Holy Ghost performs it. He who made the promise has the responsibility of keeping the promise, and He is equal to the occasion. God, who promises this marvellous change, will assuredly carry it out in all who receive Jesus, for to all such He gives power to become the Sons of God. Oh that you would believe it! Oh that you would do the gracious Lord the justice to believe that He can and will do this for you, great miracle though it will be! Oh that you would believe that God cannot lie! Oh that you would trust Him for a new heart, and a right spirit, for He can give them to you! May the Lord give you faith in His promise, faith in His Son, faith in the Holy Spirit, and faith in Him, and to Him shall be praise and honor and glory forever and ever! Amen.

BY GRACE THROUGH FAITH

"By grace are ye saved, through faith" (Ephesians 2:8).

  I THINK IT WELL to turn a little to one side that I may ask my reader to observe adoringly the fountain-head of our salvation, which is the grace of God. "By grace are ye saved." Because God is gracious, therefore sinful men are forgiven, converted, purified, and saved. It is not because of anything in them, or that ever can be in them, that they are saved; but because of the boundless love, goodness, pity, compassion, mercy, and grace of God. Tarry a moment, then, at the well-head. Behold the pure river of water of life, as it proceeds out of the throne of God and of the Lamb!
  What an abyss is the grace of God! Who can measure its breadth? Who can fathom its depth? Like all the rest of the divine attributes, it is infinite. God is full of love, for "God is love." God is full of goodness; the very name "God" is short for "good." Unbounded goodness and love enter into the very essence of the Godhead. It is because "his mercy endureth for ever" that men are not destroyed; because "his compassions fail not" that sinners are brought to Him and forgiven.
  Remember this; or you may fall into error by fixing your minds so much upon the faith which is the channel of salvation as to forget the grace which is the fountain and source even of faith itself. Faith is the work of God's grace in us. No man can say that Jesus is the Christ but by the Holy Ghost. "No man cometh unto me," saith Jesus, "except the Father which hath sent me draw him." So that faith, which is coming to Christ, is the result of divine drawing. Grace is the first and last moving cause of salvation; and faith, essential as it is, is only an important part of the machinery which grace employs. We are saved "through faith," but salvation is "by grace." Sound forth those words as with the archangel's trumpet: "By grace are ye saved." What glad tidings for the undeserving!
  Faith occupies the position of a channel or conduit pipe. Grace is the fountain and the stream; faith is the aqueduct along which the flood of mercy flows down to refresh the thirsty sons of men. It is a great pity when the aqueduct is broken. It is a sad sight to see around Rome the many noble aqueducts which no longer convey water into the city, because the arches are broken and the marvelous structures are in ruins. The aqueduct must be kept entire to convey the current; and, even so, faith must be true and sound, leading right up to God and coming right down to ourselves, that it may become a serviceable channel of mercy to our souls.
  Still, I again remind you that faith is only the channel or aqueduct, and not the fountainhead, and we must not look so much to it as to exalt it above the divine source of all blessing which lies in the grace of God. Never make a Christ out of your faith, nor think of as if it were the independent source of your salvation. Our life is found in "looking unto Jesus," not in looking to our own faith. By faith all things become possible to us; yet the power is not in the faith, but in the God upon whom faith relies. Grace is the powerful engine, and faith is the chain by which the carriage of the soul is attached to the great motive power. The righteousness of faith is not the moral excellence of faith, but the righteousness of Jesus Christ which faith grasps and appropriates. The peace within the soul is not derived from the contemplation of our own faith; but it comes to us from Him who is our peace, the hem of whose garment faith touches, and virtue comes out of Him into the soul.
  See then, dear friend, that the weakness of your faith will not destroy you. A trembling hand may receive a golden gift. The Lord's salvation can come to us though we have only faith as a grain of mustard seed. The power lies in the grace of God, and not in our faith. Great messages can be sent along slender wires, and the peace-giving witness of the Holy Spirit can reach the heart by means of a thread-like faith which seems almost unable to sustain its own weight. Think more of Him to whom you look than of the look itself. You must look away even from your own looking, and see nothing but Jesus, and the grace of God revealed in Him.

FAITH, WHAT IS IT?

WHAT IS THIS FAITH concerning which it is said, "By grace are ye saved, through faith?" There are many descriptions of faith; but almost all the definitions I have met with have made me understand it less than I did before I saw them. The Negro said, when he read the chapter, that he would confound it; and it is very likely that he did so, though he meant to expound it. We may explain faith till nobody understands it. I hope I shall not be guilty of that fault. Faith is the simplest of all things, and perhaps because of its simplicity it is the more difficult to explain.

What is faith? It is made up of three things--knowledge, belief, and trust. Knowledge comes first. "How shall they believe in him of whom they have not heard?" I want to be informed of a fact before I can possibly believe it. "Faith cometh by hearing"; we must first hear, in order that we may know what is to be believed. "They that know thy name shall put their trust in thee." A measure of knowledge is essential to faith; hence the importance of getting knowledge. "Incline your ear, and come unto me; hear, and your soul shall live." Such was the word of the ancient prophet, and it is the word of the gospel still. Search the Scriptures and learn what the Holy Spirit teacheth concerning Christ and His salvation. Seek to know God: "For he that cometh to God must believe that he is, and that he is a rewarder of them that diligently seek him." May the Holy Spirit give you the spirit of knowledge, and of the fear of the Lord! Know the gospel: know what the good news is, how it talks of free forgiveness, and of change of heart, of adoption into the family of God, and of countless other blessings. Know especially Christ Jesus the Son of God, the Saviour of men, united to us by His human nature, and yet one with God; and thus able to act as Mediator between God and man, able to lay His hand upon both, and to be the connecting link between the sinner and the Judge of all the earth. Endeavour to know more and more of Christ Jesus. Endeavour especially to know the doctrine of the sacrifice of Christ; for the point upon which saving faith mainly fixes itself is this--"God was in Christ, reconciling the world unto himself, not imputing their trespasses unto them." Know that Jesus was "made a curse for us, as it is written, Cursed is every one that hangeth on a tree." Drink deep of the doctrine of the substitutionary work of Christ; for therein lies the sweetest possible comfort to the guilty sons of men, since the Lord "made him to be sin for us, that we might be made the righteousness of God in him." Faith begins with knowledge.

The mind goes on to believe that these things are true. The soul believes that God is, and that He hears the cries of sincere hearts; that the gospel is from God; that justification by faith is the grand truth which God hath revealed in these last days by His Spirit more clearly than before. Then the heart believes that Jesus is verily and in truth our God and Saviour, the Redeemer of men, the Prophet, Priest, and King of His people. All this is accepted as sure truth, not to be called in question. I pray that you may at once come to this. Get firmly to believe that "the blood of Jesus Christ, God's dear Son, cleanseth us from all sin"; that His sacrifice is complete and fully accepted of God on man's behalf, so that he that believeth on Jesus is not condemned. Believe these truths as you believe any other statements; for the difference between common faith and saving faith lies mainly in the subjects upon which it is exercised. Believe the witness of God just as you believe the testimony of your own father or friend. "If we receive the witness of men, the witness of God is greater."

So far you have made an advance toward faith; only one more ingredient is needed to complete it, which is trust. Commit yourself to the merciful God; rest your hope on the gracious gospel; trust your soul on the dying and living Saviour; wash away your sins in the atoning blood; accept His perfect righteousness, and all is well. Trust is the lifeblood of faith; there is no saving faith without it. The Puritans were accustomed to explain faith by the word "recumbency." It meant leaning upon a thing. Lean with all your weight upon Christ. It would be a better illustration still if I said, fall at full length, and lie on the Rock of Ages. Cast yourself upon Jesus; rest in Him; commit yourself to Him. That done, you have exercised saving faith. Faith is not a blind thing; for faith begins with knowledge. It is not a speculative thing; for faith believes facts of which it is sure. It is not an unpractical, dreamy thing; for faith trusts, and stakes its destiny upon the truth of revelation. That is one way of describing what faith is.

Let me try again. Faith is believing that Christ is what He is said to be, and that He will do what He has promised to do, and then to expect this of Him. The Scriptures speak of Jesus Christ as being God, God is human flesh; as being perfect in His character; as being made of a sin-offering on our behalf; as bearing our sins in His own body on the tree. The Scripture speaks of Him as having finished transgression, made an end of sin, and brought in everlasting righteousness. The sacred records further tell us that He "rose again from the dead," that He "ever liveth to make intercession for us," that He has gone up into the glory, and has taken possession of Heaven on the behalf of His people, and that He will shortly come again "to judge the world in righteousness, and his people with equity." We are most firmly to believe that it is even so; for this is the testimony of God the Father when He said, "This is my beloved Son; hear ye him." This also is testified by God the Holy Spirit; for the Spirit has borne witness to Christ, both in the inspired Word and by divers miracles, and by His working in the hearts of men. We are to believe this testimony to be true.

Faith also believes that Christ will do what He has promised; that since He has promised to cast out none that come to Him, it is certain that He will not cast us out if we come to Him. Faith believes that since Jesus said, "The water that I shall give him shall be in him a well of water springing up into everasting life, it must be true; and if we get this living Water from Christ it will abide in us, and will well up within us in streams of holy life. Whatever Christ has promised to do He will do, and we must believe this, so as to look for pardon, justification, preservation, and eternal glory from His hands, according as He has promised them to believers in Him.

Then comes the next necessary step. Jesus is what He is said to be, Jesus will do what He says He will do; therefore we must each one trust Him, saying, "He will be to me what He says He is, and He will do to me what He has promised to do; I leave myself in the hands of Him who is appointed to save, that He may save me. I rest upon His promise that He will do even as He has said." This is a saving faith, and he that hath it hath everlasting life. Whatever his dangers and difficulties, whatever his darkness and depression, whatever his infirmities and sins, he that believeth thus on Christ Jesus is not condemned, and shall never come into condemnation.

May that explanation be of some service! I trust it may be used by the Spirit of God to direct my reader into immediate peace. "Be not afraid; only believe." Trust, and be at rest.

My fear is lest the reader should rest content with understanding what is to be done, and yet never do it. Better the poorest real faith actually at work, than the best ideal of it left in the region of speculation. The great matter is to believe on the Lord Jesus at once. Never mind distinctions and definitions. A hungry man eats though he does not understand the composition of his food, the anatomy of his mouth, or the process of digestion: he lives because he eats. Another far more clever person understands thoroughly the science of nutrition; but if he does not eat he will die, with all his knowledge. There are, no doubt, many at this hour in Hell who understood the doctrine of faith, but did not believe. On the other hand, not one who has trusted in the Lord Jesus has ever been cast out, though he may never have been able intelligently to define his faith. Oh dear reader, receive the Lord Jesus into your soul, and you shall live forever! "He that believeth in Him hath everlasting life."

HOW MAY FAITH BE ILLUSTRATED?

TO MAKE THE MATTER Of faith clearer still, I will give you a few illustrations. Though the Holy Spirit alone can make my reader see, it is my duty and my joy to furnish all the light I can, and to pray the divine Lord to open blind eyes. Oh that my reader would pray the same prayer for himself!

The faith which saves has its analogies in the human frame.
It is the eye which looks. By the eye we bring into the mind that which is far away; we can bring the sun and the far-off stars into the mind by a glance of the eye. So by trust we bring the Lord Jesus near to us; and though He be far away in Heaven, He enters into our heart. Only look to Jesus; for the hymn is strictly true--
There is life in a look at the Crucified One,
There is life at this moment for thee.

Faith is the hand which grasps. When our hand takes hold of anything for itself, it does precisely what faith does when it appropriates Christ and the blessings of His redemption. Faith says, "Jesus is mine." Faith hears of the pardoning blood, and cries, "I accept it to pardon me." Faith calls the legacies of the dying Jesus her own; and they are her own, for faith is Christ's heir; He has given Himself and all that He has to faith. Take, O friend, that which grace has provided for thee. You will not be a thief, for you have a divine permit: "Whosoever will, let him take the water of life freely." He who may have a treasure simply by his grasping it will be foolish indeed if he remains poor.

Faith is the mouth which feeds upon Christ. Before food can nourish us, it must be received into us. This is a simple matter--this eating and drinking. We willingly receive into the mouth that which is our food, and then we consent that it should pass down into our inward parts, wherein it is taken up and absorbed into our bodily frame. Paul says, in his Epistle to the Romans, in the tenth chapter, "The word is nigh thee, even in thy mouth." Now then, all that is to be done is to swallow it, to suffer it to go down into the soul. Oh that men had an appetite! For he who is hungry and sees meat before him does not need to be taught how to eat. "Give me," said one, "a knife and a fork and a chance." He was fully prepared to do the rest. Truly, a heart which hungers and thirsts after Christ has but to know that He is freely given, and at once it will receive Him. If my reader is in such a case, let him not hesitate to receive Jesus; for he may be sure that he will never be blamed for doing so: for unto "as many as received him, to them gave he power to become the sons of God." He never repulses one, but He authorizes all who come to remain sons for ever.

The pursuits of life illustrate faith in many ways. The farmer buries good seed in the earth, and expects it not only to live but to be multiplied. He has faith in the covenant arrangement, that "seed-time and harvest shall not cease," and he is rewarded for his faith.

The merchant places his money in the care of a banker, and trusts altogether to the honesty and soundness of the bank. He entrusts his capital to another's hands, and feels far more at ease than if he had the solid gold locked up in an iron safe.

The sailor trusts himself to the sea. When he swims he takes his foot from the bottom and rests upon the buoyant ocean. He could not swim if he did not wholly cast himself upon the water.

The goldsmith puts precious metal into the fire which seems eager to consume it, but he receives it back again from the furnace purified by the heat.

You cannot turn anywhere in life without seeing faith in operation between man and man, or between man and natural law. Now, just as we trust in daily life, even so are we to trust in God as He is revealed in Christ Jesus.

Faith exists in different persons in various degrees, according to the amount of their knowledge or growth in grace. Sometimes faith is little more than a simple clinging to Christ; a sense of dependence and a willingness so to depend. When you are down at the seaside you will see limpets sticking to the rock. You walk with a soft tread up to the rock; you strike the mollusk a rapid blow with your walking-stick and off he comes. Try the next limpet in that way. You have given him warning; he heard the blow with which you struck his neighbor, and he clings with all his might. You will never get him off; not you! Strike, and strike again, but you may as soon break the rock. Our little friend, the limpet, does not know much, but he clings. He is not acquainted with the geological formation of the rock, but he clings. He can cling, and he has found something to cling to: this is all his stock of knowledge, and he uses it for his security and salvation. It is the limpet's life to cling to the rock, and it is the sinner's life to cling to Jesus. Thousands of God's people have no more faith than this; they know enough to cling to Jesus with all their heart and soul, and this suffices for present peace and eternal safety. Jesus Christ is to them a Saviour strong and mighty, a Rock immovable and immutable; they cling to him for dear life, and this clinging saves them. Reader, cannot you cling? Do so at once.

Faith is seen when one man relies upon another from a knowledge of the superiority of the other. This is a higher faith; the faith which knows the reason for its dependence, and acts upon it. I do not think the limpet knows much about the rock: but as faith grows it becomes more and more intelligent. A blind man trusts himself with his guide because he knows that his friend can see, and, trusting, he walks where his guide conducts him. If the poor man is born blind he does not know what sight is; but he knows that there is such a thing as sight, and that it is possessed by his friend and therefore he freely puts his hand into the hand of the seeing one, and follows his leadership. "We walk by faith, not by sight." "Blessed are they which have not seen, and yet have believed." This is as good an image of faith as well can be; we know that Jesus has about Him merit, and power, and blessing, which we do not possess, and therefore we gladly trust ourselves to Him to be to us what we cannot be to ourselves. We trust Him as the blind man trusts his guide. He never betrays our confidence; but He "is made of God unto us wisdom, and righteousness, and sanctification, and redemption."

Every boy that goes to school has to exert faith while learning. His schoolmaster teaches him geography, and instructs him as to the form of the earth, and the existence of certain great cities and empires. The boy does not himself know that these things are true, except that he believes his teacher, and the books put into his hands. That is what you will have to do with Christ, if you are to be saved; you must simply know because He tells you, believe because He assures you it is even so, and trust yourself with Him because He promises you that salvation will be the result. Almost all that you and I know has come to us by faith. A scientific discovery has been made, and we are sure of it. On what grounds do we believe it? On the authority of certain well-known men of learning, whose reputations are established. We have never made or seen their experiments, but we believe their witness. You must do the like with regard to Jesus: because He teaches you certain truths you are to be His disciple, and believe His words; because He has performed certain acts you are to be His client, and trust yourself with Him. He is infinitely superior to you, and presents himself to your confidence as your Master and Lord. If you will receive Him and His words you shall be saved.

Another and a higher form of faith is that faith which grows out of love. Why does a boy trust his father? The reason why the child trusts his father is because he loves him. Blessed and happy are they who have a sweet faith in Jesus, intertwined with deep affection for Him, for this is a restful confidence. These lovers of Jesus are charmed with His character, and delighted with His mission, they are carried away by the lovingkindness that He has manifested, and therefore they cannot help trusting Him, because they so much admire, revere, and love Him.

The way of loving trust in the Saviour may thus be illustrated. A lady is the wife of the most eminent physician of the day. She is seized with a dangerous illness, and is smitten down by its power; yet she is wonderfully calm and quiet, for her husband has made this disease his special study, and has healed thousands who were similarly afflicted. She is not in the least troubled, for she feels perfectly safe in the hands of one so dear to her, and in whom skill and love are blended in their highest forms. Her faith is reasonable and natural; her husband, from every point of view, deserves it of her. This is the kind of faith which the happiest of believers exercise toward Christ. There is no physician like Him, none can save as He can; we love Him, and He loves us, and therefore we put ourselves into His hands, accept whatever He prescribes, and do whatever He bids. We feel that nothing can be wrongly ordered while He is the director of our affairs; for He loves us too well to let us perish, or suffer a single needless pang.

Faith is the root of obedience, and this may be clearly seen in the affairs of life. When a captain trusts a pilot to steer his vessel into port he manages the vessel according to his direction. When a traveler trusts a guide to conduct him over a difficult pass, he follows the track which his guide points out. When a patient believes in a physician, he carefully follows his prescriptions and directions. Faith which refuses to obey the commands of the Saviour is a mere pretence, and will never save the soul. We trust Jesus to save us; He gives us directions as to the way of salvation; we follow those directions and are saved. Let not my reader forget this. Trust Jesus, and prove your trust by doing whatever He bids you.

A notable form of faith arises out of assured knowledge; this comes of growth in grace, and is the faith which believes Christ because it knows Him, and trusts Him because it has proved Him to

All of Grace

be infallibly faithful. An old Christian was in the habit of writing T and P in the margin of her Bible whenever she had tried and proved a promise. How easy it is to trust a tried and proved Saviour! You cannot do this as yet, but you will do so. Everything must have a beginning. You will rise to strong faith in due time. This matured faith asks not for signs and tokens, but bravely believes. Look at the faith of the master mariner--I have often wondered at it. He looses his cable, he steams away from the land. For days, weeks, or even months, he never sees sail or shore; yet on he goes day and night without fear, till one morning he finds himself exactly opposite to the desired haven toward which he has been steering. How has he found his way over the trackless deep? He has trusted in his compass, his nautical almanac, his glass, and the heavenly bodies; and obeying their guidance, without sighting land, he has steered so accurately that he has not to change a point to enter into port. It is a wonderful thing--that sailing or steaming without sight. Spiritually it is a blessed thing to leave altogether the shores of sight and feeling, and to say, "Good-by" to inward feelings, cheering providences, signs, tokens, and so forth. It is glorious to be far out on the ocean of divine love, believing in God, and steering for Heaven straight away by the direction of the Word of God. "Blessed are they that have not seen, and yet have believed"; to them shall be administered an abundant entrance at the last, and a safe voyage on the way. Will not my reader put his trust in God in Christ Jesus. There I rest with joyous confidence. Brother, come with me, and believe our Father and our Saviour. Come at once.

WHY ARE WE SAVED BY FAITH?

WHY IS FAITH SELECTED as the channel of salvation? No doubt this inquiry is often made. "By grace are ye saved through faith," is assuredly the doctrine of Holy Scripture, and the ordinance of God; but why is it so? Why is faith selected rather than hope, or love, or patience?

It becomes us to be modest in answering such a question, for God's ways are not always to be understood; nor are we allowed presumptuously to question them. Humbly we would reply that, as far as we can tell, faith has been selected as the channel of grace, because there is a natural adaptation in faith to be used as the receiver. Suppose that I am about to give a poor man an alms: I put it into his hand--why? Well, it would hardly be fitting to put it into his ear, or to lay it upon his foot; the hand seems made on purpose to receive. So, in our mental frame, faith is created on purpose to be a receiver: it is the hand of the man, and there is a fitness in receiving grace by its means.

Do let me put this very plainly. Faith which receives Christ is as simple an act as when your child receives an apple from you, because you hold it out and promise to give him the apple if he comes for it. The belief and the receiving relate only to an apple; but they make up precisely the same act as the faith which deals with eternal salvation. What the child's hand is to the apple, that your faith is to the perfect salvation of Christ. The child's hand does not make the apple, nor improve the apple, nor deserve the apple; it only takes it; and faith is chosen by God to be the receiver of salvation, because it does not pretend to create salvation, nor to help in it, but it is content humbly to receive it. "Faith is the tongue that begs pardon, the hand which receives it, and the eye which sees it; but it is not the price which buys it." Faith never makes herself her own plea, she rests all her argument upon the blood of Christ. She becomes a good servant to bring the riches of the Lord Jesus to the soul, because she acknowledges whence she drew them, and owns that grace alone entrusted her with them.

Faith, again, is doubtless selected because it gives all the glory to God. It is of faith that it might be by grace, and it is of grace that there might be no boasting; for God cannot endure pride. "The proud he knoweth afar off," and He has no wish to come nearer to them. He will not give salvation in a way which will suggest or foster pride. Paul saith, "Not of works, lest any man should boast." Now, faith excludes all boasting. The hand which receives charity does not say, "I am to be thanked for accepting the gift"; that would be absurd. When the hand conveys bread to the mouth it does not say to the body, "Thank me; for I feed you." It is a very simple thing that the hand does though a very necessary thing; and it never arrogates glory to itself for what it does. So God has selected faith to receive the unspeakable gift of His grace, because it cannot take to itself any credit, but must adore the gracious God who is the giver of all good. Faith sets the crown upon the right head, and therefore the Lord Jesus was wont to put the crown upon the head of faith, saying, "Thy faith hath saved thee; go in peace."

Next, God selects faith as the channel of salvation because it is a sure method, linking man with God. When man confides in God, there is a point of union between them, and that union guarantees blessing. Faith saves us because it makes us cling to God, and so brings us into connection with Him. I have often used the following illustration, but I must repeat it, because I cannot think of a better. I am told that years ago a boat was upset above the falls of Niagara, and two men were being carried down the current, when persons on the shore managed to float a rope out to them, which rope was seized by them both. One of them held fast to it and was safely drawn to the bank; but the other, seeing a great log come floating by, unwisely let go the rope and clung to the log, for it was the bigger thing of the two, and apparently better to cling to. Alas! the log with the man on it went right over the vast abyss, because there was no union between the log and the shore. The size of the log was no benefit to him who grasped it; it needed a connection with the shore to produce safety. So when a man trusts to his works, or to sacraments, or to anything of that sort, he will not be saved, because there is no junction between him and Christ; but faith, though it may seem to be like a slender cord, is in the hands of the great God on the shore side; infinite power pulls in the connecting line, and thus draws the man from destruction. Oh the blessedness of faith, because it unites us to God!

Faith is chosen again, because it touches the springs of action. Even in common things faith of a certain sort lies at the root of all. I wonder whether I shall be wrong if I say that we never do anything except through faith of some sort. If I walk across my study it is because I believe my legs will carry me. A man eats because he believes in the necessity of food; he goes to business because he believes in the value of money; he accepts a check because he believes that the bank will honor it. Columbus discovered America because he believed that there was another continent beyond the ocean; and the Pilgrim Fathers colonized it because they believed that God would be with them on those rocky shores. Most grand deeds have been born of faith; for good or for evil, faith works wonders by the man in whom it dwells. Faith in its natural form is an all-prevailing force, which enters into all manner of human actions. Possibly he who derides faith in God is the man who in an evil form has the most of faith; indeed, he usually falls into a credulity which would be ridiculous, if it were not disgraceful. God gives salvation to faith, because by creating faith in us He thus touches the real mainspring of our emotions and actions. He has, so to speak, taken possession of the battery and now He can send the sacred current to every part of our nature. When we believe in Christ, and the heart has come into the possession of God, then we are saved from sin, and are moved toward repentance, holiness, zeal, prayer, consecration, and every other gracious thing. "What oil is to the wheels, what weights are to a clock, what wings are to a bird, what sails are to a ship, that faith is to all holy duties and services." Have faith, and all other graces will follow and continue to hold their course.

Faith, again, has the power of working by love; it influences the affections toward God, and draws the heart after the best things. He that believes in God will beyond all question love God. Faith is an act of the understanding; but it also proceeds from the heart. "With the heart man believeth unto righteousness"; and hence God gives salvation to faith because it resides next door to the affections, and is near akin to love; and love is the parent and the nurse of every holy feeling and act. Love to God is obedience, love to God is holiness. To love God and to love man is to be conformed to the image of Christ; and this is salvation.

Moreover, faith creates peace and joy; he that hath it rests, and is tranquil, is glad and joyous, and this is a preparation for heaven. God gives all heavenly gifts to faith, for this reason among others, that faith worketh in us the life and spirit which are to be eternally manifested in the upper and better world. Faith furnishes us with armor for this life, and education for the life to come. It enables a man both to live and to die without fear; it prepares both for action and for suffering; and hence the Lord selects it as a most convenient medium for conveying grace to us, and thereby securing us for glory.

Certainly faith does for us what nothing else can do; it gives us joy and peace, and causes us to enter into rest. Why do men attempt to gain salvation by other means? An old preacher says, "A silly servant who is bidden to open a door, sets his shoulder to it and pushes with all his might; but the door stirs not, and he cannot enter, use what strength he may. Another comes with a key, and easily unlocks the door, and enters right readily. Those who would be saved by works are pushing at heaven's gate without result; but faith is the key which opens the gate at once." Reader, will you not use that key? The Lord commands you to believe in His dear Son, therefore you may do so; and doing so you shall live. Is not this the promise of the gospel, "He that believeth and is baptized shall be saved"? (Mark 16:16). What can be your objection to a way of salvation which commends itself to the mercy and the wisdom of our gracious God?

Charles Haddon Spurgeon

ALAS! I CAN DO NOTHING!

AFTER THE ANXIOUS HEART has accepted the doctrine of atonement, and learned the great truth that salvation is by faith in the Lord Jesus, it is often sore troubled with a sense of inability toward that which is good. Many are groaning, "I can do nothing." They are not making this into an excuse, but they feel it as a daily burden. They would if they could. They can each one honestly say, "To will is present with me, but how to perform that which I would I find not."

This feeling seems to make all the gospel null and void; for what is the use of food to a hungry man if he cannot get at it? Of what avail is the river of the water of life if one cannot drink? We recall the story of the doctor and the poor woman's child. The sage practitioner told the mother that her little one would soon be better under proper treatment, but it was absolutely needful that her boy should regularly drink the best wine, and that he should spend a season at one of the German spas. This, to a widow who could hardly get bread to eat! Now, it sometimes seems to the troubled heart that the simple gospel of "Believe and live," is not, after all, so very simple; for it asks the poor sinner to do what he cannot do. To the really awakened, but half instructed, there appears to be a missing link; yonder is the salvation of Jesus, but how is it to be reached? The soul is without strength, and knows not what to do. It lies within sight of the city of refuge, and cannot enter its gate.

Is this want of strength provided for in the plan of salvation? It is. The work of the Lord is perfect. It begins where we are, and asks nothing of us in order to its completion. When the good Samaritan saw the traveler lying wounded and half dead, he did not bid him rise and come to him, and mount the ass and ride off to the inn. No, "he came where he was," and ministered to him, and lifted him upon the beast and bore him to the inn. Thus doth the Lord Jesus deal with us in our low and wretched estate.

We have seen that God justifieth, that He justifieth the ungodly and that He justifies them through faith in the precious blood of Jesus; we have now to see the condition these ungodly ones are in when Jesus works out their salvation. Many awakened persons are not only troubled about their sin, but about their moral weakness. They have no strength with which to escape from the mire into which they have fallen, nor to keep out of it in after days. They not only lament over what they have done, but over what they cannot do. They feel themselves to be powerless, helpless, and spiritually lifeless. It may sound odd to say that they feel dead, and yet it is even so. They are, in their own esteem, to all good incapable. They cannot travel the road to Heaven, for their bones are broken. "None of the men of strength have found their hands;" in fact, they are "without strength." Happily, it is written, as the commendation of God's love to us:

When we were yet without strength, in due time Christ died for the ungodly (Romans 5:6).

Here we see conscious helplessness succored--succored by the interposition of the Lord Jesus. Our helplessness is extreme. It is not written, "When we were comparatively weak Christ died for us"; or, "When we had only a little strength"; but the description is absolute and unrestricted; "When we were yet without strength." We had no strength whatever which could aid in our salvation; our Lord's words were emphatically true, "Without me ye can do nothing." I may go further than the text, and remind you of the great love wherewith the Lord loved us, "even when we were dead in trespasses and sins." To be dead is even more than to be without strength.

The one thing that the poor strengthless sinner has to fix his mind upon, and firmly retain, as his one ground of hope, is the divine assurance that "in due time Christ died for the ungodly." Believe this, and all inability will disappear. As it is fabled of Midas that he turned everything into gold by his touch, so it is true of faith that it turns everything it touches into good. Our very needs and weaknesses become blessings when faith deals with them.

Let us dwell upon certain forms of this want of strength. To begin with, one man will say, "Sir, I do not seem to have strength to collect my thoughts, and keep them fixed upon those solemn topics which concern my salvation; a short prayer is almost too much for me. It is so partly, perhaps, through natural weakness, partly because I have injured myself through dissipation, and partly also because I worry myself with wordly cares, so that I am not capable of those high thoughts which are necessary ere a soul can be saved." This is a very common form of sinful weakness. Note this! You are without strength on this point; and there are many like you. They could not carry out a train of consecutive thought to save their lives. Many poor men and women are illiterate and untrained, and these would find deep thought to be very heavy work. Others are so light and trifling by nature, that they could no more follow out a long process of argument and reasoning, than they could fly. They could never attain to the knowledge of any profound mystery if they expended their whole life in the effort. You need not, therefore, despair: that which is necessary to salvation is not continuous thought, but a simple reliance upon Jesus. Hold you on to this one fact-- "In due time Christ died for the ungodly." This truth will not require from you any deep research or profound reasoning, or convincing argument. There it stands: "In due time Christ died for the ungodly." Fix your mind on that, and rest there.

Let this one great, gracious, glorious fact lie in your spirit till it perfumes all your thoughts, and makes you rejoice even though you are without strength, seeing the Lord Jesus has become your strength and your song, yea, He has become your salvation. According to the Scriptures it is a revealed fact, that in due time Christ died for the ungodly when they were yet without strength. You have heard these words hundreds of times, maybe, and yet you have never before perceived their meaning. There is a cheering savor about them, is there not? Jesus did not die for our righteousness, but He died for our sins. He did not come to save us because we were worth the saving, but because we were utterly worthless, ruined, and undone. He came not to earth out of any reason that was in us, but solely and only out of reasons which He fetched from the depths of His own divine love. In due time He died for those whom He describes, not as godly, but as ungodly, applying to them as hopeless an adjective as He could well have selected. If you have but little mind, yet fasten it to this truth, which is fitted to the smallest capacity, and is able to cheer the heaviest heart. Let this text lie under your tongue like a sweet morsel, till it dissolves into your heart and flavors all your thoughts; and then it will little matter though those thoughts should be as scattered as autumn leaves. Persons who have never shone in science, nor displayed the least originality of mind, have nevertheless been fully able to accept the doctrine of the cross, and have been saved thereby. Why should not you?

I hear another man cry, "Oh, sir my want of strength lies mainly in this, that I cannot repent sufficiently!" A curious idea men have of what repentance is! Many fancy that so many tears are to be shed, and so many groans are to be heaved, and so much despair is to be endured. Whence comes this unreasonable notion? Unbelief and despair are sins, and therefore I do not see how they can be constituent elements of acceptable repentance; yet there are many who regard them as necessary parts of true Christian experience. They are in great error. Still, I know what they mean, for in the days of my darkness I used to feel in the same way. I desired to repent, but I thought that I could not do it, and yet all the while I was repenting. Odd as it may sound, I felt that I could not feel. I used to get into a corner and weep, because I could not weep; and I fell into bitter sorrow because I could not sorrow for sin. What a jumble it all is when in our unbelieving state we begin to judge our own condition! It is like a blind man looking at his own eyes. My heart was melted within me for fear, because I thought that my heart was as hard as an adamant stone. My heart was broken to think that it would not break. Now I can see that I was exhibiting the very thing which I thought I did not possess; but then I knew not where I was.

Oh that I could help others into the light which I now enjoy! Fain would I say a word which might shorten the time of their bewilderment. I would say a few plain words, and pray "the Comforter" to apply them to the heart.

Remember that the man who truly repents is never satisfied with his own repentance. We can no more repent perfectly than we can live perfectly. However pure our tears, there will always be some dirt in them: there will be something to be repented of even in our best repentance. But listen! To repent is to change your mind about sin, and Christ, and all the great things of God. There is sorrow implied in this; but the main point is the turning of the heart from sin to Christ. If there be this turning, you have the essence of true repentance, even though no alarm and no despair should ever have cast their shadow upon your mind.

If you cannot repent as you would, it will greatly aid you to do so if you will firmly believe that "in due time Christ died for the ungodly." Think of this again and again. How can you continue to be hard-hearted when you know that out of supreme love "Christ died for the ungodly"? Let me persuade you to reason with yourself thus: Ungodly as I am, though this heart of steel will not relent, though I smite in vain upon my breast, yet He died for such as I am, since He died for the ungodly. Oh that I may believe this and feel the power of it upon my flinty heart!

Blot out every other reflection from your soul, and sit down by the hour together, and meditate deeply on this one resplendent display of unmerited, unexpected, unexampled love, "Christ died for the ungodly." Read over carefully the narrative of the Lord's death, as you find it in the four evangelists. If anything can melt your stubborn heart, it will be a sight of the sufferings of Jesus, and the consideration that he suffered all this for His enemies.

Charles Haddon Spurgeon

> O Jesus! sweet the tears I shed, While at Thy feet I kneel,
> Gaze on Thy wounded, fainting head, And all Thy sorrows feel.
> My heart dissolves to see Thee bleed, This heart so hard before;
> I hear Thee for the guilty plead, And grief o'erflows the more.
> 'Twas for the sinful Thou didst die, And I a sinner stand:
> Convinc'd by Thine expiring eye, Slain by Thy pierced hand.

Surely the cross is that wonder-working rod which can bring water out of a rock. If you understand the full meaning of the divine sacrifice of Jesus, you must repent of ever having been opposed to One who is so full of love. It is written, "They shall look upon him whom they have pierced, and they shall mourn for him, as one mourneth for his only son, and shall be in bitterness for him, as one that is in bitterness for his firstborn." Repentance will not make you see Christ; but to see Christ will give you repentance. You may not make a Christ out of your repentance, but you must look for repentance to Christ. The Holy Ghost, by turning us to Christ, turns us from sin. Look away, then, from the effect to the cause, from your own repenting to the Lord Jesus, who is exalted on high to give repentance.

I have heard another say, "I am tormented with horrible thoughts. Wherever I go, blasphemies steal in upon me. Frequently at my work a dreadful suggestion forces itself upon me, and even on my bed I am startled from my sleep by whispers of the evil one. I cannot get away from this horrible temptation." Friend, I know what you mean, for I have myself been hunted by this wolf. A man might as well hope to fight a swarm of flies with a sword as to master his own thoughts when they are set on by the devil. A poor tempted soul, assailed by satanic suggestions, is like a traveler I have read of, about whose head and ears and whole body there came a swarm of angry bees. He could not keep them off nor escape from them. They stung him everywhere and threatened to be the death of him. I do not wonder you feel that you are without strength to stop these hideous and abominable thoughts which Satan pours into your soul; but yet I would remind you of the Scripture before us--"When we were yet without strength, in due time Christ died for the ungodly." Jesus knew where we were and where we should be; He saw that we could not overcome the prince of the power of the air; He knew that we should be greatly worried by him; but even then, when He saw us in that condition, Christ died for the ungodly. Cast the anchor of your faith upon this. The devil himself cannot tell you that you are not ungodly; believe, then, that Jesus died even for such as you are. Remember Martin Luther's way of cutting the devil's head off with his own sword. "Oh," said the devil to Martin Luther, "you are a sinner." "Yes," said he, "Christ died to save sinners." Thus he smote him with his own sword. Hide you in this refuge, and keep there: "In due time Christ died for the ungodly." If you stand to that truth, your blasphemous thoughts which you have not the strength to drive away will go away of themselves; for Satan will see that he is answering no purpose by plaguing you with them.

These thoughts, if you hate them, are none of yours, but are injections of the Devil, for which he is responsible, and not you. If you strive against them, they are no more yours than are the cursings and falsehoods of rioters in the street. It is by means of these thoughts that the Devil would drive you to despair, or at least keep you from trusting Jesus. The poor diseased woman could not come to Jesus for the press, and you are in much the same condition, because of the rush and throng of these dreadful thoughts. Still, she put forth her finger, and touched the fringe of the Lord's garment, and she was healed. Do you the same.

Jesus died for those who are guilty of "all manner of sin and blasphemy," and therefore I am sure He will not refuse those who are unwillingly the captives of evil thoughts. Cast yourself upon Him, thoughts and all, and see if He be not mighty to save. He can still those horrible whisperings of the fiend, or He can enable you to see them in their true light, so that you may not be worried by them. In His own way He can and will save you, and at length give you perfect peace. Only trust Him for this and everything else.

Sadly perplexing is that form of inability which lies in a supposed want of power to believe. We are not strangers to the cry:

> Oh that I could believe,
> Then all would easy be;
> I would, but cannot; Lord, relieve,
> My help must come from thee.

Many remain in the dark for years because they have no power, as they say, to do that which is the giving up of all power and reposing in the power of another, even the Lord Jesus. Indeed, it is a very curious thing, this whole matter of believing; for people do not get much help by trying to believe. Believing does not come by trying. If a person were to make a statement of something that happened this day, I should not tell him that I would try to believe him. If I believed in the truthfulness of the man who told the incident to me and said that he saw it, I should accept the statement at once. If I did not think him a true man, I should, of course, disbelieve him; but there would be no trying in the matter. Now, when God declares that there is salvation in Christ Jesus, I must either believe Him at once, or make Him a liar. Surely you will not hesitate as to which is the right path in this case, The witness of God must be true, and we are bound at once to believe in Jesus.

But possibly you have been trying to believe too much. Now do not aim at great things. Be satisfied to have a faith that can hold in its hand this one truth, "While we were yet without strength, in due time Christ died for the ungodly." He laid down His life for men while as yet they were not believing in Him, nor were able to believe in Him. He died for men, not as believers, but as sinners. He came to make these sinners into believers and saints; but when He died for them He viewed them as utterly without strength. If you hold to the truth that Christ died for the ungodly, and believe it, your faith will save you, and you may go in peace. If you will trust your soul with Jesus, who died for the ungodly, even though you cannot believe all things, nor move mountains, nor do any other wonderful works, yet you are saved. It is not great faith, but true faith, that saves; and the salvation lies not in the faith, but in the Christ in whom faith trusts. Faith as a grain of mustard seed will bring salvation. It is not the measure of faith, but the sincerity of faith, which is the point to be considered. Surely a man can believe what he knows to be true; and as you know Jesus to be true, you, my friend, can believe in Him.

The cross which is the object of faith, is also, by the power of the Holy Spirit, the cause of it. Sit down and watch the dying Saviour till faith springs up spontaneously in your heart. There is no place like Calvary for creating confidence. The air of that sacred hill brings health to trembling faith. Many a watcher there has said:

While I view Thee, wounded, grieving, Breathless on the cursed tree,
Lord, I feel my heart believing That Thou suffer'dst thus for me.

"Alas!" cries another, "my want of strength lies in this direction, that I cannot quit my sin, and I know that I cannot go to Heaven and carry my sin with me." I am glad that you know that, for it is quite true. You must be divorced from your sin, or you cannot be married to Christ. Recollect the question which flashed into the mind of young Bunyan when at his sports on the green on Sunday: "Wilt thou have thy sins and go to hell, or wilt thou quit thy sins and go to heaven?" That brought him to a dead stand. That is a question which every man will have to answer: for there is no going on in sin and going to heaven. That cannot be. You must quit sin or quit hope. Do you reply, "Yes, I am willing enough. To will is present with me, but how to perform that which l would I find not. Sin masters me, and I have no strength." Come, then, if you have no strength, this text is still true, "When we were yet without strength, in due time Christ died for the ungodly." Can you still believe that? However other things may seem to contradict it, will you believe it? God has said it, and it is a fact; therefore, hold on to it like grim death, for your only hope lies there. Believe this and trust Jesus, and you shall soon find power with which to slay your sin; but apart from Him, the strong man armed will hold you for ever his bond slave. Personally, I could never have overcome my own sinfulness. I tried and failed. My evil propensities were too many for me, till, in the belief that Christ died for me, I cast my guilty soul on Him, and then I received a conquering principle by which I overcame my sinful self. The doctrine of the cross can be used to slay sin, even as the old warriors used their huge two- handed swords, and mowed down their foes at every stroke. There is nothing like faith in the sinner's Friend: it overcomes all evil. If Christ has died for me, ungodly as I am, without strength as I am, then I cannot live in sin any longer, but must arouse myself to love and serve Him who hath redeemed me. I cannot trifle with the evil which slew my best Friend. I must be holy for His sake. How can I live in sin when He has died to save me from it?

See what a splendid help this is to you that are without strength, to know and believe that in due time Christ died for such ungodly ones as you are. Have you caught the idea yet? It is, somehow, so difficult for our darkened, prejudiced, and unbelieving minds to see the essence of the gospel. At times I have thought, when I have done preaching, that I have laid down the gospel so clearly, that the nose on one's face could not be more plain; and yet I perceive that even intelligent hearers have failed to understand what was meant by "Look unto me and be ye saved." Converts usually say that they did not know the gospel till such and such a day; and yet they had heard it for years. The gospel is unknown, not from want of explanation, but from absence of personal revelation. This the Holy Ghost is ready to give, and will give to those who ask Him. Yet when given, the sum total of the truth revealed all lies within these words: "Christ died for the ungodly."

I hear another bewailing himself thus: "Oh, sir, my weakness lies in this, that I do not seem to keep long in one mind! I hear the word on a Sunday, and I am impressed; but in the week I meet with an evil companion, and my good feelings are all gone. My fellow workmen do not believe in anything, and they say such terrible things, and I do not know how to answer them, and so I find myself knocked over." I know this Plastic Pliable very well, and I tremble for him; but at the same time, if he is really sincere, his weakness can be met by divine grace. The Holy Spirit can cast out the evil spirit of the fear of man. He can make the coward brave. Remember, my poor vacillating friend, you must not remain in this state. It will never do to be mean and beggarly to yourself. Stand upright, and look at yourself, and see if you were ever meant to be like a toad under a harrow, afraid for your life either to move or to stand still. Do have a mind of your own. This is not a spiritual matter only, but one which concerns ordinary manliness. I would do many things to please my friends; but to go to hell to please them is more than I would venture. It may be very well to do this and that for good fellowship; but it will never do to lose the friendship of God in order to keep on good terms with men. "I know that," says the man, "but still, though I know it, I cannot pluck up courage. I cannot show my colors. I cannot stand fast." Well, to you also I have the same text to bring: "When we were yet without strength, in due time Christ died for the ungodly." If Peter were here, he would say, "The Lord Jesus died for me even when I was such a poor weak creature that the maid who kept the fire drove me to lie, and to swear that I knew not the Lord." Yes, Jesus died for those who forsook him and fled. Take a firm grip on this truth--"Christ died for the ungodly while they were yet without strength." This is your way out of your cowardice. Get this wrought into your soul, "Christ died for me," and you will soon be ready to die for Him. Believe it, that He suffered in your place and stead, and offered for you a full, true, and satisfactory expiation. If you believe that fact, you will be forced to feel, "I cannot be ashamed of Him who died for me." A full conviction that this is true will nerve you with a dauntless courage. Look at the saints in the martyr age. In the early days of Christianity, when this great thought of Christ's exceeding love was sparkling in all its freshness in the church, men were not only ready to die, but they grew ambitious to suffer, and even presented themselves by hundreds at the judgment seats of the rulers, confessing the Christ. I do not say that they were wise to court a cruel death; but it proves my point, that a sense of the love of Jesus lifts the mind above all fear of what man can do to us. Why should it not produce the same effect in you? Oh that it might now inspire you with a brave resolve to come out upon the Lord's side, and be His follower to the end!

May the Holy Spirit help us to come thus far by faith in the Lord Jesus, and it will be well!

THE INCREASE OF FAITH

HOW CAN WE OBTAIN an increase of faith? This is a very earnest question to many. They say they want to believe, but cannot. A great deal of nonsense is talked upon this subject. Let us be strictly practical in our dealing with it. Common sense is as much needed in religion as anywhere else. "What am I to do in order to believe?" One who was asked the best way to do a certain simple act, replied that the best way to do it was to do it at once. We waste time in discussing methods when the action is simple. The shortest way to believe is to believe. If the Holy Spirit has made you candid, you will believe as soon as truth is set before you. You will believe it because it is true. The gospel command is clear; "Believe in the Lord Jesus Christ, and thou shalt be saved." It is idle to evade this by questions and quibbles. The order is plain; let it be obeyed.

But still, if you have difficulty, take it before God in prayer. Tell the great Father exactly what it is that puzzles you, and beg Him by His Holy Spirit to solve the question. If I cannot believe a statement in a book, I am glad to inquire of the author what he means by it; and if he is a true man his explanation will satisfy me; much more will the divine explanation of the hard points of Scripture satisfy the heart of the true seeker. The Lord is willing to make himself known; go to Him and see if it is not so. Repair at once to your closet, and cry, "O Holy Spirit, lead me into the truth! What I know not, teach Thou me."

Furthermore, if faith seems difficult, it is possible that God the Holy Spirit will enable you to believe if you hear very frequently and earnestly that which you are commanded to believe. We believe many things because we have heard them so often. Do you not find it so in common life, that if you hear a thing fifty times a day, at last you come to believe it? Some men have come to believe very unlikely statements by this process, and therefore I do not wonder that the good Spirit often blesses the method of often hearing the truth, and uses it to work faith concerning that which is to be believed. It is written, "Faith cometh by hearing"; therefore hear often. If I earnestly and attentively hear the gospel, one of these days I shall find myself believing that which I hear, through the blessed operation of the Spirit of God upon my mind. Only mind you hear the gospel, and do not distract your mind with either hearing or reading that which is designed to stagger you.

If that, however, should seem poor advice, I would add next, consider the testimony of others. The Samaritans believed because of what the woman told them concerning Jesus. Many of our beliefs arise out of the testimony of others. I believe that there is such a country as Japan; I never saw it, and yet I believe that there is such a place because others have been there. I believe that I shall die; I have never died, but a great many have done so whom I once knew, and therefore I have a conviction that I shall die also. The testimony of many convinces me of that fact. Listen, then, to those who tell you how they were saved, how they were pardoned, how they were changed in character. If you will look into the matter you will find that somebody just like yourself has been saved. If you have been a thief, you will find that a thief rejoiced to wash away his sin in the fountain of Christ's blood. If unhappily you have been unchaste, you will find that men and women who have fallen in that way have been cleansed and changed. If you are in despair, you have only to get among God's people, and inquire a little, and you will discover that some of the saints have been equally in despair at times and they will be pleased to tell you how the Lord delivered them. As you listen to one after another of those who have tried the word of God, and proved it, the divine Spirit will lead you to believe. Have you not heard of the African who was told by the missionary that water sometimes became so hard that a man could walk on it? He declared that he believed a great many things the missionary had told him; but he would never believe that. When he came to England it came to pass that one frosty day he saw the river frozen, but he would not venture on it. He knew that it was a deep river, and he felt certain that he would be drowned if he ventured upon it. He could not be induced to walk the frozen water till his friend and many others went upon it; then he was persuaded, and trusted himself where others had safely ventured. So, while you see others believe in the Lamb of God, and notice their joy and peace, you will yourself be gently led to believe. The experience of others is one of God's ways of helping us to faith. You have either to believe in Jesus or die; there is no hope for you but in Him.

A better plan is this--note the authority upon which you are commanded to believe, and this will greatly help you to faith. The authority is not mine, or you might well reject it. But you are commanded to believe upon the authority of God himself. He bids you believe in Jesus Christ, and you must not refuse to obey your Maker. The foreman of a certain works had often heard the gospel, but he was troubled with the fear that he might not come to Christ. His good master one day sent a card around to the works--"Come to my house immediately after work." The foreman appeared at his master's door, and the master came out, and said somewhat roughly, "What do you want, John, troubling me at this time? Work is done, what right have you here?" "Sir," said he, "I had a card from you saying that I was to come after work." "Do you mean to say that merely because you had a card from me you are to come up to my house and call me out after business hours?" "Well, Sir," replied the foreman, "I do not understand you, but it seems to me that, as you sent for me, I had a right to come." "Come in, John," said his master, "I have another message that I want to read to you," and he sat down and read these words: "Come unto me, all ye that labor and are heavy laden, and I will give you rest." "Do you think after such a message from Christ that you can be wrong in coming to him?" The poor man saw it all at once, and believed in the Lord Jesus unto eternal life, because he perceived that he had good warrant and authority for believing. So have you, poor soul! You have good authority for coming to Christ, for the Lord himself bids you trust Him.

If that does not breed faith in you, think over what it is that you have to believe--that the Lord Jesus Christ suffered in the place and stead of sinners, and is able to save all who trust Him. Why, this is the most blessed fact that ever men were told to believe; the most suitable, the most comforting, the most divine truth that was ever set before mortal minds. I advise you to think much upon it, and search out the grace and love which it contains. Study the four Evangelists, study Paul's epistles, and then see if the message is not such a credible one that you are forced to believe it.

If that does not do, then think upon the person of Jesus Christ--think of who He is, and what He did, and where He is, and what He is. How can you doubt Him? It is cruelty to distrust the ever truthful Jesus. He has done nothing to deserve distrust; on the contrary, it should be easy to rely upon Him. Why crucify Him anew by unbelief? Is not this crowning Him with thorns again, and spitting upon Him again? What! is He not to be trusted? What worse insult did the soldiers pour upon Him than this? They made Him a martyr; but you make Him a liar--this is worse by far. Do not ask how can I believe? But answer another question--How can you disbelieve?

If none of these things avail, then there is something wrong about you altogether, and my last word is, submit yourself to God! Prejudice or pride is at the bottom of this unbelief. May the Spirit of God take away your enmity and make you yield. You are a rebel, a proud rebel, and that is why you do not believe your God. Give up your rebellion; throw down your weapons; yield at discretion, surrender to your King. I believe that never did a soul throw up its hands in self-despair, and cry, "Lord, I yield," but what faith became easy to it before long. It is because you still have a quarrel with God, and resolve to have your own will and your own way, that therefore you cannot believe. "How can ye believe," said Christ, "that have honor one of another?" Proud self creates unbelief. Submit, O man. Yield to your God, and then shall you sweetly believe in your Saviour. May the Holy Ghost now work secretly but effectually with you, and bring you at this very moment to believe in the Lord Jesus! Amen.

REGENERATION AND THE HOLY SPIRIT

YE MUST BE BORN AGAIN." This word of our Lord Jesus has appeared to flame in the way of many, like the drawn sword of the cherub at the gate of Paradise. They have despaired, because this change is beyond their utmost effort. The new birth is from above, and therefore it is not in the creature's power. Now, it is far from my mind to deny, or ever to conceal, a truth in order to create a false comfort. I freely admit that the new birth is supernatural, and that it cannot be wrought by the sinner's own self. It would be a poor help to my reader if I were wicked enough to try to cheer him by persuading him to reject or forget what is unquestionably true.

But is it not remarkable that the very chapter in which our Lord makes this sweeping declaration also contains the most explicit statement as to salvation by faith? Read the third chapter of John's Gospel and do not dwell alone upon its earlier sentences. It is true that the third verse says:

Jesus answered and said unto him, Verily, verily, I say unto thee, Except a man be born again, he cannot see the kingdom of God.

But, then, the fourteenth and fifteenth verses speak:

And as Moses lifted up the serpent in the wilderness, even so must the Son of man be lifted up: that whosoever believeth in him should not perish, but have eternal life.

The eighteenth verse repeats the same doctrine in the broadest terms:

He that believeth on him is not condemned: but he that believeth not is condemned already, because he hath not believed in the name of the only begotten Son of God.

It is clear to every reader that these two statements must agree, since they came from the same lips, and are recorded on the same inspired page. Why should we make a difficulty where there can be none? If one statement assures us of the necessity to salvation of a something, which only God can give, and if another assures us that the Lord will save us upon our believing in Jesus, then we may safely conclude that the Lord will give to those who believe all that is declared to be necessary to salvation. The Lord does, in fact, produce the new birth in all who believe in Jesus; and their believing is the surest evidence that they are born again.

We trust in Jesus for what we cannot do ourselves: if it were in our own power, what need of looking to Him? It is ours to believe, it is the Lord's to create us anew. He will not believe for us, neither are we to do regenerating work for Him. It is enough for us to obey the gracious command; it is for the Lord to work the new birth in us. He who could go so far as to die on the cross for us, can and will give us all things that are needful for our eternal safety.

"But a saving change of heart is the work of the Holy Spirit." This also is most true, and let it be far from us to question it, or to forget it. But the work of the Holy Spirit is secret and mysterious, and it can only be perceived by its results. There are mysteries about our natural birth into which it would be an unhallowed curiosity to pry: still more is this the case with the sacred operations of the Spirit of God. "The wind bloweth where it listeth, and thou hearest the sound thereof, but canst not tell whence it cometh, or whither it goeth; so is every one that is born of the Spirit." This much, however, we do know--the mysterious work of the Holy Spirit cannot be a reason for refusing to believe in Jesus to whom that same Spirit beareth witness.

If a man were bidden to sow a field, he could not excuse his neglect by saying that it would be useless to sow unless God caused the seed to grow. He would not be justified in neglecting tillage because the secret energy of God alone can create a harvest. No one is hindered in the ordinary pursuits of life by the fact that unless the Lord build the house they labor in vain that build it. It is certain that no man who believes in Jesus will ever find that the Holy Spirit refuses to work in him: in fact, his believing is the proof that the Spirit is already at work in his heart.

God works in providence, but men do not therefore sit still. They could not move without the divine power giving them life and strength, and yet they proceed upon their way without question; the power being bestowed from day to day by Him in whose hand their breath is, and whose are all their ways. So is it in grace. We repent and believe, though we could do neither if the Lord did not enable us. We forsake sin and trust in Jesus, and then we perceive that the Lord has wrought in us to will and to do of His own good pleasure. It is idle to pretend that there is any real difficulty in the matter.

Some truths which it is hard to explain in words are simple enough in actual experience. There is no discrepancy between the truth that the sinner believes, and that his faith is wrought in him by the Holy Spirit. Only folly can lead men to puzzle themselves about plain matters while their souls are in danger. No man would refuse to enter a lifeboat because he did not know the specific gravity of bodies; neither would a starving man decline to eat till he understood the whole process of mutrition. If you, my reader, will not believe till you can understand all mysteries, you will never be saved at all; and if you allow self- invented difficulties to keep you from accepting pardon through your Lord and Saviour, you will perish in a condemnation which will be richly deserved. Do not commit spiritual suicide through a passion for discussing metaphysical subtleties.

"MY REDEEMER LIVETH"

CONTINUALLY have I spoken to the reader concerning Christ crucified, who is the great hope of the guilty; but it is our wisdom to remember that our Lord has risen from the dead and lives eternally.

You are not asked to trust in a dead Jesus, but in One who, though He died for our sins, has risen again for our justification. You may go to Jesus at once as to a living and present friend. He is not a mere memory, but a continually existent Person who will hear your prayers and answer them. He lives on purpose to carry on the work for which He once laid down His life. He is interceding for sinners at the right hand of the Father, and for this reason He is able to save them to the uttermost who come unto God by Him. Come and try this living Saviour, if you have never done so before.

This living Jesus is also raised to an eminence of glory and power. He does not now sorrow as "a humble man before his foes," nor labor as "the carpenter's son"; but He is exalted far above principalities and power and every name that is named. The Father has given Him all power in Heaven and in earth, and he exercises this high endowment in carrying out His work of grace. Hear what Peter and the other apostles testified concerning Him before the high priest and the council:

The God of our fathers raised up Jesus, whom ye slew and hanged on a tree. Him hath God exalted with his right hand to be a Prince and a Saviour, for to give repentance to Israel, and forgiveness of sins (Acts 5:30, 31).

The glory which surrounds the ascended Lord should breathe hope into every believer's breast. Jesus is no mean person--He is "a Saviour and a great one." He is the crowned and enthroned Redeemer of men. The sovereign prerogative of life and death is vested in Him; the Father has put all men under the mediatorial government of the Son, so that He can quicken whom He will. He openeth, and no man shutteth. At His word the soul which is bound by the cords of sin and condemnation can be unloosed in a moment. He stretches out the silver scepter, and whosoever touches it lives.

It is well for us that as sin lives, and the flesh lives, and the devil lives, so Jesus lives; and it is also well that whatever might these may have to ruin us, Jesus has still greater power to save us.

All His exaltation and ability are on our account. "He is exalted to be," and exalted "to give." He is exalted to be a Prince and a Saviour, that He may give all that is needed to accomplish the salvation of all who come under His rule. Jesus has nothing which He will not use for a sinner's salvation, and He is nothing which He will not display in the aboundings of His grace. He links His princedom with His Saviour-ship, as if He would not have the one without the other; and He sets forth His exaltation as designed to bring blessings to men, as if this were the flower and crown of His glory. Could anything be more calculated to raise the hopes of seeking sinners who are looking Christward?

Jesus endured great humiliation, and therefore there was room for Him to be exalted. By that humiliation He accomplished and endured all the Father's will, and therefore He was rewarded by being raised to glory. He uses that exaltation on behalf of His people. Let my reader raise his eyes to these hills of glory, whence his help must come. Let him contemplate the high glories of the Prince and Saviour. Is it not most hopeful for men that a Man is now on the throne of the universe? Is it not glorious that the Lord of all is the Saviour of sinners? We have a Friend at court; yea, a Friend on the throne. He will use all His influence for those who entrust their affairs in His hands. Well does one of our poets sing:

He ever lives to intercede
Before His Father's face;
Give Him, my soul, Thy cause to plead,
No doubt the Father's grace.

Come, friend, and commit your cause and your case to those once pierced hands, which are now glorified with the signet rings of royal power and honor. No suit ever failed which was left with this great Advocate.

REPENTANCE MUST GO WITH FORGIVENESS

IT IS CLEAR from the text which we have lately quoted that repentance is bound up with the forgiveness of sins. In Acts 5:31 we read that Jesus is "exalted to give repentance and forgiveness of sins." These two blessings come from that sacred hand which once was nailed to the tree, but is now raised to glory. Repentance and forgiveness are riveted together by the eternal purpose of God. What God hath joined together let no man put asunder.

Repentance must go with remission, and you will see that it is so if you think a little upon the matter. It cannot be that pardon of sin should be given to an impenitent sinner; this were to confirm him in his evil ways, and to teach him to think little of evil. If the Lord were to say, "You love sin, and live in it, and you are going on from bad to worse, but, all the same, I forgive you," this were to proclaim a horrible license for iniquity. The foundations of social order would be removed, and moral anarchy would follow. I cannot tell what innumerable mischiefs would certainly occur if you could divide repentance and forgiveness, and pass by the sin while the sinner remained as fond of it as ever. In the very nature of things, if we believe in the holiness of God, it must be so, that if we continue in our sin, and will not repent of it, we cannot be forgiven, but must reap the consequence of our obstinacy. According to the infinite goodness of God, we are promised that if we will forsake our sins, confessing them, and will, by faith, accept the grace which is provided in Christ Jesus, God is faithful and just to forgive us our sins, and to cleanse us from all unrighteousness. But, so long as God lives, there can be no promise of mercy to those who continue in their evil ways, and refuse to acknowledge their wrongdoing. Surely no rebel can expect the King to pardon his treason while he remains in open revolt. No one can be so foolish as to imagine that the Judge of all the earth will put away our sins if we refuse to put them away ourselves.

Moreover, it must be so for the completeness of divine mercy. That mercy which could forgive the sin and yet let the sinner live in it would be scant and superficial mercy. It would be unequal and deformed mercy, lame upon one of its feet, and withered as to one of its hands. Which, think you, is the greater privilege, cleansing from the guilt of sin, or deliverance from the power of sin? I will not attempt to weigh in the scales two mercies so surpassing. Neither of them could have come to us apart from the precious blood of Jesus. But it seems to me that to be delivered from the dominion of sin, to be made holy, to be made like to God, must be reckoned the greater of the two, if a comparison has to be drawn. To be forgiven is an immeasurable favor. We make this one of the first notes of our psalm of praise: "Who forgiveth all thine iniquities." But if we could be forgiven, and then could be permitted to love sin, to riot in iniquity, and to wallow in lust, what would be the use of such a forgiveness? Might it not turn out to be a poisoned sweet, which would most effectually destroy us? To be washed, and yet to lie in the mire; to be pronounced clean, and yet to have the leprosy white on one's brow, would be the veriest mockery of mercy. What is it to bring the man out of his sepulcher if you leave him dead? Why lead him into the light if he is still blind? We thank God, that He who forgives our iniquities also heals our diseases. He who washes us from the stains of the past also uplifts us from the foul ways of the present, and keeps us from failing in the future. We must joyfully accept both repentance and remission; they cannot be separated. The covenant heritage is one and indivisible, and must not be parceled out. To divide the work of grace would be to cut the living child in halves, and those who would permit this have no interest in it.

I will ask you who are seeking the Lord, whether you would be satisfied with one of these mercies alone? Would it content you, my reader, if God would forgive you your sin and then allow you to be as worldly and wicked as before? Oh, no! The quickened spirit is more afraid of sin itself than of the penal results of it. The cry of your heart is not, "Who shall deliver me from punishment?" but, "O wretched man that I am! Who shall deliver me from the body of this death? Who shall enable me to live above temptation, and to become holy, even as God is holy?" Since the unity of repentance with remission agrees with gracious desire, and since it is necessary for the completeness of salvation, and for holiness' sake, rest you sure that it abides.

Repentance and forgiveness are joined together in the experience of all believers. There never was a person yet who did unfeignedly repent of sin with believing repentance who was not forgiven; and on the other hand, there never was a person forgiven who had not repented of his sin. I do not hesitate to say that beneath the copes of Heaven there never was, there is not, and there never will be, any case of sin being washed away, unless at the same time the heart was led to repentance and faith in Christ. Hatred of sin and a sense of pardon come together into the soul, and abide together while we live.

These two things act and react upon each other: the man who is forgiven, therefore repents; and the man who repents is also most assuredly forgiven. Remember first, that forgiveness leads to repentance. As we sing in Hart's words:

Law and terrors do but harden,
All the while they work alone;
But a sense of blood-bought pardon
Soon dissolves a heart of stone.

When we are sure that we are forgiven, then we abhor iniquity; and I suppose that when faith grows into full assurance, so that we are certain beyond a doubt that the blood of Jesus has washed us whiter than snow, it is then that repentance reaches to its greatest height. Repentance grows as faith grows. Do not make any mistake about it; repentance is not a thing of days and weeks, a temporary penance to be over as fast as possible! No; it is the grace of a lifetime, like faith itself. God's little children repent, and so do the young men and the fathers. Repentance is the inseparable companion of faith. All the while that we walk by faith and not by sight, the tear of repentance glitters in the eye of faith. That is not true repentance which does not come of faith in Jesus, and that is not true faith in Jesus which is not tinctured with repentance. Faith and repentance, like Siamese twins, are vitally joined together. In proportion as we believe in the forgiving love of Christ, in that proportion we repent; and in proportion as we repent of sin and hate evil, we rejoice in the fullness of the absolution which Jesus is exalted to bestow. You will never value pardon unless you feel repentance; and you will never taste the deepest draught of repentance until you know that you are pardoned. It may seem a strange thing, but so it is--the bitterness of repentance and the sweetness of pardon blend in the flavor of every gracious life, and make up an incomparable happiness.

These two covenant gifts are the mutual assurance of each other. If I know that I repent, I know that I am forgiven. How am I to know that I am forgiven except I know also that I am turned from my former sinful course? To be a believer is to be a penitent. Faith and repentance are but two spokes in the same wheel, two handles of the same plough. Repentance has been well described as a heart broken for sin, and from sin; and it may equally well be spoken of as turning and returning. It is a change of mind of the most thorough and radical sort, and it is attended with sorrow for the past, and a resolve of amendment in the future.

Repentance is to leave
The sins we loved before;
And show that we in earnest grieve,
By doing so no more.

Now, when that is the case, we may be certain that we are forgiven; for the Lord never made a heart to be broken for sin and broken from sin, without pardoning it. If, on the other hand, we are enjoying pardon, through the blood of Jesus, and are justified by faith, and have peace with God, through Jesus Christ our Lord, we know that our repentance and faith are of the right sort.

Do not regard your repentance as the cause of your remission, but as the companion of it. Do not expect to be able to repent until you see the grace of our Lord Jesus, and His readiness to blot out your sin. Keep these blessed things in their places, and view them in their relation to each other. They are the Jachin and Boaz of a saving experience; I mean that they are comparable to Solomon's two great pillars which stood in the forefront of the house of the Lord, and formed a majestic entrance to the holy place. No man comes to God aright except he passes between the pillars of repentance and remission. Upon your heart the rainbow of covenant grace has been displayed in all its beauty when the tear-drops of repentance have been shone upon by the light of full forgiveness. Repentance of sin and faith in divine pardon are the warp and woof of the fabric of real conversion. By these tokens shall you know an Israelite indeed.

To come back to the Scripture upon which we are meditating: both forgiveness and repentance flow from the same source, and are given by the same Saviour. The Lord Jesus in His glory bestows both upon the same persons. You are neither to find the remission nor the repentance elsewhere. Jesus has both ready, and He is prepared to bestow them now, and to bestow them most freely on all who will accept them at His hands. Let it never be forgotten that Jesus gives all that is needful for our salvation. It is highly important that all seekers after mercy should remember this. Faith is as much the gift of God as is the Saviour upon whom that faith relies. Repentance of sin is

All of Grace

as truly the work of grace as the making of an atonement by which sin is blotted out. Salvation, from first to last, is of grace alone. You will not misunderstand me. It is not the Holy Spirit who repents. He has never done anything for which He should repent. If He could repent, it would not meet the case; we must ourselves repent of our own sin, or we are not saved from its power. It is not the Lord Jesus Christ who repents. What should He repent of? We ourselves repent with the full consent of every faculty of our mind. The will, the affections, the emotions, all work together most heartily in the blessed act of repentance for sin; and yet at the back of all that is our personal act, there is a secret holy influence which melts the heart, gives contrition, and produces a complete change. The Spirit of God enlightens us to see what sin is, and thus makes it loathsome in our eyes. The Spirit of God also turns us toward holiness, makes us heartily to appreciate, love, and desire it, and thus gives us the impetus by which we are led onward from stage to stage of sanctification. The Spirit of God works in us to will and to do according to God's good pleasure. To that good Spirit let us submit ourselves at once, that He may lead us to Jesus, who will freely give us the double benediction of repentance and remission, according to the riches of His grace.

"BY GRACE ARE YE SAVED."

HOW REPENTANCE IS GIVEN

TO RETURN to the grand text: "Him hath God exalted with his right hand to be a Prince and a Saviour, for to give repentance to Israel, and forgiveness of sins." Our Lord Jesus Christ has gone up that grace may come down. His glory is employed to give greater currency to His grace. The Lord has not taken a step upward except with the design of bearing believing sinners upward with Him. He is exalted to give repentance; and this we shall see if we remember a few great truths.

The work which our Lord Jesus has done has made repentance possible, available, and acceptable. The law makes no mention of repentance, but says plainly, "The soul that sinneth, it shall die." If the Lord Jesus had not died and risen again and gone unto the Father, what would your repenting or mine be worth? We might feel remorse with its horrors, but never repentance with its hopes. Repentance, as a natural feeling, is a common duty deserving no great praise: indeed, it is so generally mingled with a selfish fear of punishment, that the kindliest estimate makes but little of it. Had not Jesus interposed and wrought out a wealth of merit, our tears of repentance would have been so much water spilled upon the ground. Jesus is exalted on high, that through the virtue of His intercession repentance may have a place before God. In this respect He gives us repentance, because He puts repentance into a position of acceptance, which otherwise it could never have occupied.

When Jesus was exalted on high, the Spirit of God was poured out to work in us all needful graces. The Holy Ghost creates repentance in us by supernaturally renewing our nature, and taking away the heart of stone out of our flesh. Oh, sit not down straining those eyes of yours to fetch out impossible tears! Repentance comes not from unwilling nature, but from free and sovereign grace. Get not to your chamber to smite your breast in order to fetch from a heart of stone feelings which are not there. But go to Calvary and see how Jesus died. Look upward to the hills whence comes your help. The Holy Ghost has come on purpose that He may overshadow men's spirits and breed repentance within them, even as once He brooded over chaos and brought forth order. Breathe your prayer to Him, "Blessed Spirit, dwell with me. Make me tender and lowly of heart, that I may hate sin and unfeignedly repent of it." He will hear your cry and answer you.

Remember, too, that when our Lord Jesus was exalted, He not only gave us repentance by sending forth the Holy Spirit, but by consecrating all the works of nature and of providence to the great ends of our salvation, so that any one of them may call us to repentance, whether it crow like Peter's cock, or shake the prison like the jailer's earthquake. From the right hand of God our Lord Jesus rules all things here below, and makes them work together for the salvation of His redeemed. He uses both bitters and sweets, trials and joys, that He may produce in sinners a better mind toward their God. Be thankful for the providence which has made you poor, or sick, or sad; for by all this Jesus works the life of your spirit and turns you to Himself. The Lord's mercy often rides to the door of our hearts on the black horse of affliction. Jesus uses the whole range of our experience to wean us from earth and woo us to Heaven. Christ is exalted to the throne of Heaven and earth in order that, by all the processes of His providence, He may subdue hard hearts unto the gracious softening of repentance.

Besides, He is at work at this hour by all His whispers in the conscience, by His inspired Book, by those of us who speak out of that Book, and by praying friends and earnest hearts. He can send a word to you which shall strike your rocky heart as with the rod of Moses, and cause streams of repentance to flow forth. He can bring to your mind some heart-breaking text out of Holy Scripture which shall conquer you right speedily. He can mysteriously soften you, and cause a holy frame of mind to steal over you when you least look for it. Be sure of this, that He who is gone into His glory, raised into all the splendor and majesty of God, has abundant ways of working repentance in those to whom He grants forgiveness. He is even now waiting to give repentance to you. Ask Him for it at once.

Observe with much comfort that the Lord Jesus Christ gives this repentance to the most unlikely people in the world. He is exalted to give repentance to Israel. To Israel! In the days when the apostles thus spoke, Israel was the nation which had most grossly sinned against light and love, by daring to say, "His blood be on us and on our children." Yet Jesus is exalted to give them repentance! What a marvel of grace! If you have been brought up in the brightest of Christian light,

All of Grace

and yet have rejected it, there is still hope. If you have sinned against conscience, and against the Holy Spirit, and against the love of Jesus, there is yet space for repentance. Though you may be as hard as unbelieving Israel of old, softening may yet come to you, since Jesus is exalted, and clothed with boundless power. For those who went the furthest in iniquity, and sinned with special aggravation, the Lord Jesus is exalted to give to them repentance and forgiveness of sins. Happy am I to have so full a gospel to proclaim! Happy are you to be allowed to read it!

The hearts of the children of Israel had grown hard as an adamant stone. Luther used to think it impossible to convert a Jew. We are far from agreeing with him, and yet we must admit that the seed of Israel have been exceedingly obstinate in their rejection of the Saviour during these many centuries. Truly did the Lord say, "Israel would none of me." "He came to his own and his own received him not." Yet on behalf of Israel our Lord Jesus is exalted for the giving of repentance and remission. Probably my reader is a Gentile; but yet he may have a very stubborn heart, which has stood out against the Lord Jesus for many years; and yet in him our Lord can work repentance. It may be that you will yet feel compelled to write as William Hone did when he yielded to divine love. He was the author of those most entertaining volumes called the "Everyday Book," but he was once a stout-hearted infidel. When subdued by sovereign grace, he wrote:

The proudest heart that ever beat
Hath been subdued in me;
The wildest will that ever rose
To scorn Thy cause and aid Thy foes
Is quell'd my Lord, by Thee.
Thy will, and not my will be done,
My heart be ever Thine;
Confessing Thee the mighty Word,
My Saviour Christ, my God, my Lord,
Thy cross shall be my sign.

The Lord can give repentance to the most unlikely, turning lions into lambs, and ravens into doves. Let us look to Him that this great change may be wrought in us. Assuredly the contemplation of the death of Christ is one of the surest and speediest methods of gaining repentance. Do not sit down and try to pump up repentance from the dry well of corrupt nature. It is contrary to the laws of mind to suppose that you can force your soul into that gracious state. Take your heart in prayer to Him who understands it, and say, "Lord, cleanse it. Lord, renew it. Lord, work repentance in it." The more you try to produce penitent emotions in yourself, the more you will be disappointed; but if you believingly think of Jesus dying for you, repentance will burst forth. Meditate on the Lord's shedding His heart's blood out of love to you. Set before your mind's eye the agony and bloody sweat, the cross and passion; and, as you do this, He who was the bearer of all this grief will look at you, and with that look He will do for you what He did for Peter, so that you also will go out and weep bitterly. He who died for you can, by His gracious Spirit, make you die to sin; and He who has gone into glory on your behalf can draw your soul after Him, away from evil, and toward holiness.

I shall be content if I leave this one thought with you; look not beneath the ice to find fire, neither hope in your own natural heart to find repentance. Look to the Living One for life. Look to Jesus for all you need between Hell Gate and Heaven Gate. Never seek elsewhere for any part of that which Jesus loves to bestow; but remember, Christ is all.

THE FEAR OF FINAL FALLING

A DARK FEAR haunts the minds of many who are coming to Christ; they are afraid that they shall not persevere to the end. I have heard the seeker say: "If I were to cast my soul upon Jesus, yet peradventure I should after all draw back into perdition. I have had good feelings before now, and they have died away. My goodness has been as the morning cloud, and as the early dew. It has comeon a sudden, lasted for a season, promised much, and then vanished away."

I believe that this fear is often the father of the fact; and that some who have been afraid to trust Christ for all time, and for all eternity, have failed because they had a temporary faith, which never went far enough to save them. They set out trusting to Jesus in a measure, but looking to themselves for continuance and perseverance in the heavenward way; and so they set out faultily, and, as a natural consequence, turned back before long. If we trust to ourselves for our holding on we shall not hold on. Even though we rest in Jesus for a part of our salvation, we shall fail if we trust to self for anything. No chain is stronger than its weakest link: if Jesus be our hope for everything, except one thing, we shall utterly fail, because in that one point we shall come to nought. I have no doubt whatever that a mistake about the perseverance of the saints has prevented the perseverance of many who did run well. What did hinder them that they should not continue to run? They trusted to themselves for that running, and so they stopped short. Beware of mixing even a little of self with the mortar with which you build, or you will make it untempered mortar, and the stones will not hold together. If you look to Christ for your beginnings, beware of looking to yourself for your endings. He is Alpha. See to it that you make Him Omega also. If you begin in the Spirit you must not hope to be made perfect by the flesh. Begin as you mean to go on, and go on as you began, and let the Lord be all in all to you. Oh, that God, the Holy Spirit, may give us a very clear idea of where the strength must come from by which we shall be preserved until the day of our Lord's appearing!

Here is what Paul once said upon this subject when he was writing to the Corinthians:

Our Lord Jesus Christ, who shall also confirm you unto the end, that ye may be blameless in the day of our Lord Jesus Christ. God is faithful, by whom ye were called unto the fellowship of his Son Jesus Christ our Lord (1 Cor. 1:8, 9).

This language silently admits a great need, by telling us how it is provided for. Wherever the Lord makes a provision, we are quite sure that there was a need for it, since no superfluities encumber the covenant of grace. Golden shields hung in Solomon's courts which were never used, but there are none such in the armory of God. What God has provided we shall surely need. Between this hour and the consummation of all things every promise of God and every provision of the covenant of grace will be brought into requisition. The urgent need of the believing soul is confirmation, continuance, final perseverance, preservation to the end. This is the great necessity of the most advanced believers, for Paul was writing to saints at Corinth, who were men of a high order, of whom he could say, "I thank my God always on your behalf, for the grace of God which is given you by Jesus Christ." Such men are the very persons who most assuredly feel that they have daily need of new grace if they are to hold on, and hold out, and come off conquerors at the last. If you were not saints you would have no grace, and you would feel no need of more grace; but because you are men of God, therefore you feel the daily demands of the spiritual life. The marble statue requires no food; but the living man hungers and thirsts, and he rejoices that his bread and his water are made sure to him, for else he would certainly faint by the way. The believer's personal wants make it inevitable that he should daily draw from the great source of all supplies; for what could he do if he could not resort to his God?

This is true of the most gifted of the saints--of those men at Corinth who were enriched with all utterance and with all knowledge. They needed to be confirmed to the end, or else their gifts and attainments would prove their ruin. If we had the tongues of men and of angels, if we did not receive fresh grace, where should we be? If we had all experience till we were fathers in the church--if we had been taught of God so as to understand all mysteries--yet we could not live a single day without the divine life flowing into us from our Covenant Head. How could we hope to

All of Grace

hold on for a single hour, to say nothing of a lifetime, unless the Lord should hold us on? He who began the good work in us must perform it unto the day of Christ, or it will prove a painful failure.

This great necessity arises very much from our own selves. In some there is a painful fear that they shall not persevere in grace because they know their own fickleness. Certain persons are constitutionally unstable. Some men are by nature conservative, not to say obstinate; but others are as naturally variable and volatile. Like butterflies they flit from flower to flower, till they visit all the beauties of the garden, and settle upon none of them. They are never long enough in one place to do any good; not even in their business nor in their intellectual pursuits. Such persons may well be afraid that ten, twenty, thirty, forty, perhaps fifty years of continuous religious watchfulness will be a great deal too much for them. We see men joining first one church and then another, till they box the compass. They are everything by turns and nothing long. Such have double need to pray that they may be divinely confirmed, and may be made not only steadfast but unmoveable, or otherwise they will not be found "always abounding in the work of the Lord."

All of us, even if we have no constitutional temptation to fickleness, must feel our own weakness if we are really quickened of God. Dear reader, do you not find enough in any one single day to make you stumble? You that desire to walk in perfect holiness, as I trust you do; you that have set before you a high standard of what a Christian should be--do you not find that before the breakfast things are cleared away from the table, you have displayed enough folly to make you ashamed of yourselves? If we were to shut ourselves up in the lone cell of a hermit, temptation would follow us; for as long as we cannot escape from ourselves we cannot escape from incitements to sin. There is that within our hearts which should make us watchful and humble before God. If he does not confirm us, we are so weak that we shall stumble and fall; not overturned by an enemy, but by our own carelessness. Lord, be thou our strength. We are weakness itself.

Besides that, there is the weariness which comes of a long life. When we begin our Christian profession we mount up with wings as eagles, further on we run without weariness; but in our best and truest days we walk without fainting. Our pace seems slower, but it is more serviceable and better sustained. I pray God that the energy of our youth may continue with us so far as it is the energy of the Spirit and not the mere fermentation of proud flesh. He that has long been on the road to Heaven finds that there was good reason why it was promised that his shoes should be iron and brass, for the road is rough. He has discovered that there are Hills of Difficulty and Valleys of Humiliation; that there is a Vale of Deathshade, and, worse still, a Vanity Fair--and all these are to be traversed. If there be Delectable Mountains (and, thank God, there are,) there are also Castles of Despair, the inside of which pilgrims have too often seen. Considering all things, those who hold out to the end in the way of holiness will be "men wondered at."

"O world of wonders, I can say no less." The days of a Christian's life are like so many Koh-i-noors of mercy threaded upon the golden string of divine faithfulness. In Heaven we shall tell to angels, and principalities, and powers, the unsearchable riches of Christ which were spent upon us, and enjoyed by us while we were here below. We have been kept alive on the brink of death. Our spiritual life has been a flame burning on in the midst of the sea, a stone that has remained suspended in the air. It will amaze the universe to see us enter the pearly gate, blameless in the day of our Lord Jesus Christ. We ought to be full of grateful wonder if kept for an hour; and I trust we are.

If this were all, there would be enough cause for anxiety; but there is far more. We have to think of what a place we live in. The world is a howling wilderness to many of God's people. Some of us are greatly indulged in the providence of God, but others have a stern fight of it. We begin our day with prayer, and we hear the voice of holy song full often in our houses; but many good people have scarcely risen from their knees in the morning before they are saluted with blasphemy. They go out to work, and all day long they are vexed with filthy conversation like righteous Lot in Sodom. Can you even walk the open streets without your ears being afflicted with foul language? The world is no friend to grace. The best we can do with this world is to get through it as quickly as we can, for we dwell in an enemy's country. A robber lurks in every bush. Everywhere we need to travel with a "drawn sword" in our hand, or at least with that weapon which is called all-prayer ever at our side; for we have to contend for every inch of our way. Make no mistake about this, or you will be rudely shaken out of your fond delusion. O God, help us, and confirm us to the end, or where shall we be?

True religion is supernatural at its beginning, supernatural in its continuance, and supernatural in its close. It is the work of God from first to last. There is great need that the hand of the Lord should be stretched out still: that need my reader is feeling now, and I am glad that he should feel it; for now he will look for his own preservation to the Lord who alone is able to keep us from failing, and glorify us with His Son.

CONFIRMATION

I WANT YOU TO NOTICE the security which Paul confidently expected for all the saints. He says--"Who shall confirm you unto the end, that ye may be blameless in the day of our Lord Jesus Christ." This is the kind of confirmation which is above all things to be desired. You see it supposes that the persons are right, and it proposes to confirm them in the right. It would be an awful thing to confirm a man in ways of sin and error. Think of a confirmed drunkard, or a confirmed thief, or a confirmed liar. It would be a deplorable thing for a man to be confirmed in unbelief and ungodliness. Divine confirmation can only be enjoyed by those to whom the grace of God has been already manifested. It is the work of the Holy Ghost. He who gives faith strengthens and establishes it: He who kindles love in us preserves it and increases its flame. What He makes us to know by His first teaching, the good Spirit causes us to know with greater clearness and certainty by still further instruction. Holy acts are confirmed till they become habits, and holy feelings are confirmed till they become abiding conditions. Experience and practice confirm our beliefs and our resolutions. Both our joys and our sorrows, our successes and our failures, are sanctified to the selfsame end: even as the tree is helped to root itself both by the soft showers and the rough winds. The mind is instructed, and in its growing knowledge it gathers reasons for persevering in the good way: the heart is comforted, and so it is made to cling more closely to the consoling truth. The grip grows tighter, and the tread grows firmer, and the man himself becomes more solid and substantial.

This is not a merely natural growth, but is as distinct a work of the Spirit as conversion. The Lord will surely give it to those who are relying upon Him for eternal life. By His inward working He will deliver us from being "unstable as water," and cause us to be rooted and grounded. It is a part of the method by which He saves us--this building us up into Christ Jesus and causing us to abide in Him. Dear reader, you may daily look for this; and you shall not be disappointed. He whom you trust will make you to be as a tree planted by the rivers of waters, so preserved that even your leaf shall not wither.

What a strength to a church is a confirmed Christian! He is a comfort to the sorrowful, and a help to the weak. Would you not like to be such? Confirmed believers are pillars in the house of our God. These are not carried away by every wind of doctrine, nor overthrown by sudden temptation. They are a great stay to others, and act as anchors in the time of church trouble. You who are beginning the holy life hardly dare to hope that you will become like them. But you need not fear; the good Lord will work in you as well as in them. One of these days you who are now a "babe" in Christ shall be a "father" in the church. Hope for this great thing; but hope for it as a gift of grace, and not as the wages of work, or as the product of your own energy.

The inspired apostle Paul speaks of these people as to be confirmed unto the end. He expected the grace of God to preserve them personally to the end of their lives, or till the Lord Jesus should come. Indeed, he expected that the whole church of God in every place and in all time would be kept to the end of the dispensation, till the Lord Jesus as the Bridegroom should come to celebrate the wedding-feast with his perfected Bride. All who are in Christ will be confirmed in Him till that illustrious day. Has He not said, "Because I live ye shall live also"? He also said, "I give unto my sheep eternal life; and they shall never perish, neither shall any man pluck them out of my hand." He that hath begun a good work in you will confirm it unto the day of Christ. The work of grace in the soul is not a superficial reformation; the life implanted as the new birth comes of a living and incorruptible seed, which liveth and abideth for ever; and the promises of God made to believers are not of a transient character, but involve for their fulfilment the believer's holding on his way till he comes to endless glory. We are kept by the power of God, through faith unto salvation. "The righteous shall hold on his way." Not as the result of our own merit or strength, but as a gift of free and undeserved favor those who believe are "preserved in Christ Jesus." Of the sheep of His fold Jesus will lose none; no member of His Body shall die; no gem of His treasure shall be missing in the day when He makes up His jewels. Dear reader, the salvation which is received by faith is not a thing of months and years; for our Lord Jesus hath "obtained eternal salvation for us," and that which is eternal cannot come to an end.

Paul also declares his expectation that the Corinthian saints would be "Confirmed to the end blameless." This blamelessness is a precious part of our keeping. To be kept holy is better than

All of Grace

merely to be kept safe. It is a dreadful thing when you see religious people blundering out of one dishonor into another; they have not believed in the power of our Lord to make them blameless. The lives of some professing Christians are a series of stumbles; they are never quite down, and yet they are seldom on their feet. This is not a fit thing for a believer; he is invited to walk with God, and by faith he can attain to steady perseverance in holiness; and he ought to do so. The Lord is able, not only to save us from hell, but to keep us from falling. We need not yield to temptation. Is it not written, "Sin shall not have dominion over you?" The Lord is able to keep the feet of His saints; and He will do it if we will trust Him to do so. We need not defile our garments, we may by His grace keep them unspotted from the world; we are bound to do this, "for without holiness no man shall see the Lord."

The apostle prophesied for these believers, that which he would have us seek after--that we may be preserved, blameless unto the day of our Lord Jesus Christ." The revised version has "unreproveable," instead of "blameless." Possibly a better rendering would be "unimpeachable." God grant that in that last great day we may stand free from all charge, that none in the whole universe may dare to challenge our claim to be the redeemed of the Lord. We have sins and infirmities to mourn over, but these are not the kind of faults which would prove us to be out of Christ; we shall be clear of hypocrisy, deceit, hatred, and delight in sin; for these things would be fatal charges. Despite our failings, the Holy Spirit can work in us a character spotless before men; so that, like Daniel, we shall furnish no occasion for accusing tongues, except in the matter of our religion. Multitudes of godly men and women have exhibited lives so transparent, so consistent throughout, that none could gainsay them. The Lord will be able to say of many a believer, as he did of Job, when Satan stood before Him, "Hast thou considered my servant, a perfect and an upright man, one that feareth God and escheweth evil?" This is what my reader must look for at the Lord's hands. This is the triumph of the saints--to continue to follow the Lamb whithersoever He goeth, maintaining our integrity as before the living God. May we never turn aside into crooked ways, and give cause to the adversary to blaspheme. Of the true believer it is written, "He keepeth himself, and that wicked one toucheth him not." May it be so written concerning us!

Friend just beginning in the divine life, the Lord can give you an irreproachable character. Even though in your past life you may have gone far into sin, the Lord can altogether deliver you from the power of former habits, and make you an example of virtue. He can not only make you moral, but He can make you abhor every false way and follow after all that is saintly. Do not doubt it. The chief of sinners need not be a whit behind the purest of the saints. Believe for this, and according to your faith shall it be unto you.

Oh, what a joy it will be to be found blameless in the day of judgment! We sing not amiss, when we join in that charming hymn:

Bold shall I stand in that great day,
For who aught to my charge shall lay;
While through Thy blood absolved I am,
From sin's tremendous curse and shame?

What bliss it will be to enjoy that dauntless courage, when heaven and earth shall flee away from the face of the Judge of all! This bliss shall be the portion of everyone who looks alone to the grace of God in Christ Jesus, and in that sacred might wages continual war with all sin.

WHY SAINTS PERSEVERE

THE HOPE which filled the heart of Paul concerning the Corinthian brethren we have already seen to be full of comfort to those who trembled as to their future. But why was it that he believed that the brethren would be confirmed unto the end?

I want you to notice that he gives his reasons. Here they are:

God is faithful, by whom ye were called unto the fellowship of his Son Jesus Christ (1 Cor. 1:9).

The apostle does not say, "You are faithful." Alas! the faithfulness of man is a very unreliable affair; it is mere vanity. He does not say, "You have faithful ministers to lead and guide you, and therefore I trust you will be safe." Oh, no! if we are kept by men we shall be but ill kept. He puts it, "God is faithful." If we are found faithful, it will be because God is faithful. On the faithfulness of our covenant God the whole burden of our salvation must rest. On this glorious attribute of God the matter hinges. We are variable as the wind, frail as a spider's web, weak as water. No dependence can be placed upon our natural qualities, or our spiritual attainments; but God abideth faithful. He is faithful in His love; He knows no variableness, neither shadow of turning. He is faithful to His purpose; He doth not begin a work and then leave it undone. He is faithful to His relationships; as a Father He will not renounce His children, as a friend He will not deny His people, as a Creator He will not forsake the work of His own hands. He is faithful to His promises, and will never allow one of them to fail to a single believer. He is faithful to His covenant, which He has made with us in Christ Jesus, and ratified with the blood of His sacrifice. He is faithful to His Son, and will not allow His precious blood to be spilled in vain. He is faithful to His people to whom He has promised eternal life, and from whom He will not turn away.

This faithfulness of God is the foundation and cornerstone of our hope of final perseverance. The saints shall persevere in holiness, because God perseveres in grace. He perseveres to bless, and therefore believers persevere in being blessed. He continues to keep His people, and therefore they continue to keep His commandments. This is good solid ground to rest upon, and it is delightfully consistent with the title of this little book, "all of grace." Thus it is free favor and infinite mercy which ring in the dawn of salvation, and the same sweet bells sound melodiously through the whole day of grace.

You see that the only reasons for hoping that we shall be confirmed to the end, and be found blameless at the last, are found in our God; but in Him these reasons are exceedingly abundant.

They lie first, in what God has done. He has gone so far in blessing us that it is not possible for Him to run back. Paul reminds us that He has "called us into the fellowship of his Son Jesus Christ." Has he called us? Then the call cannot be reversed; for, "the gifts and calling of God are without repentance." From the effectual call of His grace the Lord never turns. "Whom he called them he also justified, and whom he justified them he also glorified:" this is the invariable rule of the divine procedure. There is a common call, of which it is said, "Many are called, but few are chosen," but this of which we are now thinking is another kind of call, which betokens special love, and necessitates the possession of that to which we are called. In such a case it is with the called one even as with Abraham's seed, of whom the Lord said, "I have called thee from the ends of the earth, and said unto thee, Thou art my servant; I have chosen thee, and not cast thee away."

In what the Lord has done, we see strong reasons for our preservation and future glory, because the Lord has called us into the fellowship of His Son Jesus Christ. It means into partnership with Jesus Christ, and I would have you carefully consider what this means. If you are indeed called by divine grace, you have come into fellowship with the Lord Jesus Christ, so as to be joint-owner with Him in all things. Henceforth you are one with Him in the sight of the Most High. The Lord Jesus bare your sins in His own body on the tree, being made a curse for you; and at the same time He has become your righteousness, so that you are justified in Him. You are Christ's and Christ is yours. As Adam stood for his descendants, so does Jesus stand for all who are in Him. As husband and wife are one, so is Jesus one with all those who are united to Him by faith; one by a conjugal union which can never be broken. More than this, believers are members of the Body of

All of Grace

Christ, and so are one with Him by a loving, living, lasting union. God has called us into this union, this fellowship, this partnership, and by this very fact He has given us the token and pledge of our being confirmed to the end. If we were considered apart from Christ we should be poor perishable units, soon dissolved and borne away to destruction; but as one with Jesus we are made partakers of His nature, and are endowed with His immortal life. Our destiny is linked with that of our Lord, and until He can be destroyed it is not possible that we should perish.

Dwell much upon this partnership with the Son of God, unto which you have been called: for all your hope lies there. You can never be poor while Jesus is rich, since you are in one firm with Him. Want can never assail you, since you are joint-proprietor with Him who is Possessor of Heaven and earth. You can never fail; for though one of the partners in the firm is as poor as a church mouse, and in himself an utter bankrupt, who could not pay even a small amount of his heavy debts, yet the other partner is inconceivably, inexhaustibly rich. In such partnership you are raised above the depression of the times, the changes of the future, and the shock of the end of all things. The Lord has called you into the fellowship of His Son Jesus Christ, and by that act and deed He has put you into the place of infallible safeguard.

If you are indeed a believer you are one with Jesus, and therefore you are secure. Do you not see that it must be so? You must be confirmed to the end until the day of His appearing, if you have indeed been made one with Jesus by the irrevocable act of God. Christ and the believing sinner are in the same boat: unless Jesus sinks, the believer will never drown. Jesus has taken His redeemed into such connection with himself, that He must first be smitten, overcome, and dishonored, ere the least of His purchased ones can be injured. His name is at the head of the firm, and until it can be dishonored we are secure against all dread of failure.

So, then, with the utmost confidence let us go forward into the unknown future, linked eternally with Jesus. If the men of the world should cry, "Who is this that cometh up from the wilderness, leaning upon her Beloved?" we will joyfully confess that we do lean on Jesus, and that we mean to lean on Him more and more. Our faithful God is an everflowing well of delight, and our fellowship with the Son of God is a full river of joy. Knowing these glorious things we cannot be discouraged: nay, rather we cry with the apostle, "Who shall separate us from the love of God which is in Christ Jesus our Lord?"

CLOSE

IF MY READER has not followed me step by step as he has read my pages, I am truly sorry. Book-reading is of small value unless the truths which pass before the mind are grasped, appropriated, and carried out to their practical issues. It is as if one saw plenty of food in a shop and yet remained hungry, for want of personally eating some. It is all in vain, dear reader, that you and I have met, unless you have actually laid hold upon Christ Jesus, my Lord. On my part there was a distinct desire to benefit you, and I have done my best to that end. It pains me that I have not been able to do you good, for I have longed to win that privilege. I was thinking of you when I wrote this page, and I laid down my pen and solemnly bowed my knee in prayer for everyone who should read it. It is my firm conviction that great numbers of readers will get a blessing, even though you refuse to be of the number. But why should you refuse? If you do not desire the choice blessing which I would have brought to you, at least do me the justice to admit that the blame of your final doom will not lie at my door. When we two meet before the great white throne you will not be able to charge me with having idly used the attention which you were pleased to give me while you were reading my little book. God knoweth I wrote each line for your eternal good. I now in spirit take you by the hand. I give you a firm grip. Do you feel my brotherly grasp? The tears are in my eyes as I look at you and say, Why will you die? Will you not give your soul a thought? Will you perish through sheer carelessness? Oh, do not so; but weigh these solemn matters, and make sure work for eternity! Do not refuse Jesus, His love, His blood, His salvation. Why should you do so? Can you do it?

I beseech you,

Do not turn away from your Redeemer!

If, on the other hand, my prayers are heard, and you, my reader, have been led to trust the Lord Jesus and receive from Him salvation by grace, then keep you ever to this doctrine, and this way of living. Let Jesus be your all in all, and let free grace be the one line in which you live and move. There is no life like that of one who lives in the favor of God. To receive all as a free gift preserves the mind from self-righteous pride, and from self-accusing despair. It makes the heart grow warm with grateful love, and thus it creates a feeling in the soul which is infinitely more acceptable to God than anything that can possibly come of slavish fear. Those who hope to be saved by trying to do their best know nothing of that glowing fervor, that hallowed warmth, that devout joy in God, which come with salvation freely given according to the grace of God. The slavish spirit of self-salvation is no match for the joyous spirit of adoption. There is more real virtue in the least emotion of faith than in all the tuggings of legal bond-slaves, or all the weary machinery of devotees who would climb to Heaven by rounds of ceremonies. Faith is spiritual, and God who is a spirit delights in it for that reason. Years of prayer-saying, and church-going, or chapel-going, and ceremonies, and performances, may only be an abomination in the sight of Jehovah; but a glance from the eye of true faith is spiritual and it is therefore dear to Him. "The Father seeketh such to worship him." Look you first to the inner man, and to the spiritual, and the rest will then follow in due course.

If you are saved yourself, be on the watch for the souls of others. Your own heart will not prosper unless it is filled with intense concern to bless your fellow men. The life of your soul lies in faith; its health lies in love. He who does not pine to lead others to Jesus has never been under the spell of love himself. Get to the work of the Lord--the work of love. Begin at home. Visit next your neighbors. Enlighten the village or the street in which you live. Scatter the word of the Lord wherever your hand can reach.

Reader, meet me in heaven! Do not go down to hell. There is no coming back again from that abode of misery. Why do you wish to enter the way of death when Heaven's gate is open before you? Do not refuse the free pardon, the full salvation which Jesus grants to all who trust Him. Do not hesitate and delay. You have had enough of resolving, come to action. Believe in Jesus now, with full and immediate decision. Take with you words and come unto your Lord this day, even this day. Remember, O soul, it may be now or never with you. Let it be NOW; it would be horrible that it should be never.

Again I charge you, meet me in heaven.

Made in the USA
Monee, IL
28 April 2026